YOU DECIDE

YOU DECIDE

Using Living Wills
and Other Advance Directives
to Guide Your Treatment Choices

Evelyn J. Van Allen

Irwin Professional Publishing
Burr Ridge, Illinois
New York, New York

American Hospital Publishing, Inc.
Chicago, Illinois

This publication is designed to provide accurate and
authoritative information in regard to the subject matter
covered. It is sold with the understanding that neither the
author nor the publisher is engaged in rendering legal, accounting,
or other professional service. If legal advice or other expert
assistance is required, the services of a competent
professional person should be sought.

From a Declaration of Principles jointly adopted by a Committee
of the American Bar Association and a Committee of Publishers.

Sponsoring editor: Jean Marie Geracie
Project editor: Gladys True
Production manager: Ann Cassady
Compositor: BookMakers
Typeface: 11/13 Times Roman
Printer: Arcata Graphics/Kingsport

344.0419
V 217y

Library of Congress Cataloging-in-Publication Data

Van Allen, Evelyn J.
    You decide : using living wills and other advance directives to
guide your treatment choices / Evelyn J. Van Allen.
        p.   cm.
    Includes bibliographic references.
    ISBN 1-55623-936-X
    1. Right to die—Law and legislation—United States—Popular
works.   I. Title.
KF3827.E87V36   1994
344.73'04197—dc20
[347.3044197   93–16867

Printed in the United States of America
1 2 3 4 5 6 7 8 9 0 AGK 0 9 8 7 6 5 4 3

PREFACE

Do you have a living will or other advance directive? You will be asked this question if you are admitted to a hospital or nursing home, receive home health or hospice care, or enroll in a health maintenance organization (HMO). Most people do not have an advance directive; many intend to write one but don't know where or how to begin. Some have a directive but aren't sure if it will be honored in their state, by their doctor, or by their family. The purpose of this book is to provide some practical advice for anyone who is thinking about preparing an advance directive.

What is an advance directive? It is a written statement, an instruction, about the kind of medical treatment you want if you are not able to make treatment decisions for yourself or a document saying that you want the person named to make such decisions on your behalf. The first type of directive is typically called a *living will;* the second, either a *durable power of attorney agreement for health care* or a *health care proxy designation.* You can make both types. We'll discuss the advantages and disadvantages of each in Chapter 3.

A living will is *not* about money and property. Financial wills, unlike living wills, go into effect after death, and different laws apply to them. We will discuss some financial issues in Chapter 7, but advance directives for medical treatment are the primary focus of this book. Both medical treatment directives and financial directives, such as property wills and trusts, are important documents that can help to guide those who must make important decisions on your behalf. Most people have neither a medical nor a financial directive. The young woman who cut my hair this morning is an exception. She said, "Before our first child was born, my husband and I decided we'd better take care of all these things in advance in case something should happen to either of us." It's unusual to find someone as young as she who has prepared a living will, much less both a living will and a property will.

Advance directives are important for people of all ages. Two of the most publicized right-to-die court cases, those of Karen Ann Quinlan and Nancy Cruzan, involved young women in their 20s. Neither had written a directive about her wishes related to life-sustaining treatment, so the courts became the decision makers, and their families suffered through a long, painful public process. At this writing, a young woman named Christine

Busalacchi is in the same Missouri Care Center as was Nancy Cruzan, also the victim of an automobile accident. The accident occurred seven years ago when Christine was 16 years old. It left her in a persistent vegetative state, which means that she has no conscious brain function, as we will discuss in Chapter 1. Neither the hospital nor the courts will honor her father's request to stop the tube feeding that is keeping her alive, nor will they allow him to move her to another state where the law would permit it. Christine was not old enough to have prepared a directive under Missouri law. Even if the law had permitted it, it would have been most unusual for one so young to have contemplated death and dying and prepared an advance directive.

This book is for people of all ages who are willing to think about the last days and months of their lives, about death and dying. Many people can't or won't do so. I think of a man who overheard my conversation with a nurse about living wills. (This conversation took place in a laundromat when we were both doing vacation laundry—a reminder that discussions of life, death, and living wills often take place in ordinary places, not necessarily in doctors' or lawyers' offices, hospitals, churches, temples, or mosques.) Our eavesdropper said, "I could never make out a living will—I can't bear to think about something as awful as my death." I asked him how he intended to have medical decisions made for him if he could not make them himself. He turned pale, thought a moment, and said, "My wife will make them." I then asked, "How will she know what you want? Won't it be hard for her to decide?" He walked away.

We can't walk away from death and dying, but we can have some control over the kind of medical treatment that we receive at the end of our lives. Most of us, if asked, would have some general notion about what we want or do not want. "I don't want (or I do want) heroic measures used just to keep me alive." "I want ordinary but not extraordinary care." "I want to die with dignity." The problem with such statements is that they leave much to interpretation—and disagreement. Treatment that seems extraordinary today may be ordinary, and customary, tomorrow. Cardiopulmonary resuscitation (CPR) is an example of customary treatment, as we'll discuss in Chapter 4.

On the other hand, most of us are not medical experts. Even if we were, it would be impossible to know every medical condition and every medical treatment that we might encounter. Some will say, "Doctors and nurses should be able to make decisions about what is best, because they've cared for people who are dying. They should know the best way to care for me." Certainly, health care providers are skilled and compassionate, but they cannot know the extent of treatment that you or I really want when we are terminally ill. An advance directive is our way to guide them, to communicate our wishes, to exercise our right to self-determination.

The Congress of the United States felt that directives are so important that it passed a law in 1990 to strengthen patients' awareness of their right to prepare an advance directive and to assure that such directives are honored by health care providers. Senator John Danforth of Missouri, Republican, and Senator Daniel Patrick Moynihan of New York, Democrat, introduced the law, which is called the Patient Self-Determination Act (PSDA). It had bipartisan support, showing widespread public concern about patients' rights and decisions on life-sustaining treatment. This law, which went into effect December 1, 1991, is the reason you will be asked if you have a living will or other advance directive in many health care situations. If you have a directive, it must be placed in your medical record. The PSDA also requires hospitals, nursing homes, home health agencies, hospices, and HMOs to provide you with written information about your right to participate in health care decisions, including the right to refuse treatment. They must also give you information about your state's law on advance directives and their own policies related to advance directives and provide staff and community education about these directives. All these requirements must be carried out as part of the providers' duties under their Medicare and Medicaid Participation Agreements. The law does not apply directly to physicians, however, so it is especially important that you talk with your doctor about your advance directive.

Even though the PSDA is a powerful incentive for preparing an advance directive, the directive should be prepared long before you are hospitalized, enter a nursing home, or begin home health or hospice care. Preparing a directive is a thoughtful process; it should not be done hurriedly. We'll discuss this process in Chapter 3.

Other laws also apply to advance directives and patients' rights to participate in treatment decisions. Forty-three states and the District of Columbia now have living will laws; some of them also provide for appointing a *proxy* or *surrogate* (substitute) decision maker. Many states have durable power of attorney for health care laws; some also have separate family or proxy decision laws.

The United States Constitution, through interpretation by various state courts and one U.S. Supreme Court decision, also influences medical decision making at the end of life. In fact, the courts have probably been the most influential force in recent years—a reflection of the power that fear and misunderstanding of civil and criminal law wields in our society. This legalistic approach to the care of dying people is compounded because we continue to develop more treatments for more diseases but have not arrived at consensus as to how, when, and why they should be used. This uncertainty forces decisions—decisions that once were made at the bedside, guided by compassion and common sense—into the legal arena.

The philosophical, moral, and religious beliefs and emotional needs of each individual involved in caring for a dying person also play an important role in medical treatment decisions. The law may say that the patient is the primary decision maker, but there are many forces—some unrecognized, others unchallenged—that can make it difficult for patients to have their wishes honored. Individual doctors and nurses have their own personal values and religious beliefs about death and about their duty to provide medical treatment. One family member may not be able to let go and may persuade the caregivers to "try a bit longer." Or there may be disagreement as to the benefits or burdens of a specific treatment. For example, a doctor or a family member may feel that a 10 percent, 20 percent, or 50 percent chance for benefit is reason for treatment; others may want 75 percent or 90 percent. And doctors cannot guarantee that a particular treatment will benefit a particular patient; they can only use their best judgment, based on their experience in the treatment of others. Doctors may disagree among themselves, or with the family, that the patient's condition is terminal. Or families, as well as doctors and nurses, may not be sure what the patient would want.

How can we anticipate these roadblocks, these impediments, to a "natural" death? The answer is that we can't remove all uncertainty, but by preparing an advance directive, we can assist those who must make medical decisions for us when we are unable to do so. Preparing an advance directive is a responsible act, undertaken on behalf of others as well as ourselves. It is not an easy task.

My purpose in writing this book is to share some experiences and insights acquired during eight years as a bioethics consultant involved in education and legislation related to advance directives. During this time, I have spoken at more than 100 living will programs, many of them sponsored by senior citizens' groups. I have learned from the questions, comments, and experiences shared by participants in these programs and will, in turn, share them with you.

Life experiences—the death of a husband, caring for parents and parents-in-law through their aging and deaths—also have provided emotional and practical lessons about medical decisions at the end of life. And finally, the arduous but satisfying task of preparing, and later revising, my own living will prompts me to write this book in hopes that it will be of practical assistance to others.

The first two chapters provide general information about advance directives and some of the ethical and legal considerations related to medical decision making and the role of advance directives. This information will be helpful when preparing a directive, because it places the directive in perspective. An advance directive is not a medical order; it is not absolute assurance that treatment will or will not be provided in accordance with our wishes. As we shall learn, advance directives are based on well-recognized, generally accepted ethical principles, on constitutional, statutory, and common law, and on medical practice. The power of an advance directive, however, has a more practical basis—its communication value. In Chapters 3 through 5, we go through the process of preparing an advance directive. In Chapter 7 we look at some financial considerations, including preparing a financial directive—a property will or living trust—and health insurance.

Some readers may be tempted to ignore the first part of the book, to "just get the job done," as one man who phoned for advice about preparing his declaration in Minnesota said. Minnesota's living will law requires all declarations to be substantially the same as the form in the law. The form is long and somewhat redundant and asks those who prepare a declaration to state their wishes about "appropriate health care," "life-sustaining treatment," and "artificially administered sustenance." Some find it overwhelming, as did this man. He said, "I've had this form for two months, and nobody will tell me what to write in all these (blankety-blank) blanks." I replied that I would not tell him what to write because a living will must reflect the declarant's wishes, not someone else's. I did share some examples from my own living will, explaining that they were based on my own values, beliefs, and wishes. He said, "Not so fast, I want to write these down," and I had the uncomfortable feeling that he was simply copying my words onto his form. I trust that if you decide to prepare an advance directive, you will spend time reflecting on your own values, experiences, and beliefs. Doing so will enhance the communication value, and the power, of your directive.

Evelyn J. Van Allen

ACKNOWLEDGMENTS

Many people have contributed in many ways to this book: Audrey Kaufman of the American Hospital Association, who first suggested a guide to assist persons to prepare an advance directive; Jean Geracie, acquisitions editor, Business One Irwin, whose advice and persistence made it happen; Ronald Cranford, M.D., for clinical review of the information on persistent vegetative state and his encouraging words about the need for a consumer-oriented guide; John Eichenlaub, physician and friend, for his advice and counsel; my daughter, Pamela Larson, who reviewed and commented on innumerable drafts of the manuscript; my husband, Edward, not only for reviewing the manuscript but for granting me shore leave to write it, Barbara Frank for providing a quiet place ashore for me to write.

I also wish to acknowledge the contributions of those whose efforts to pass Minnesota's Living Will Act provided the opportunity for me to participate in both legislative and educational efforts: the Minnesota Network for Institutional Ethics Committee; the Minnesota Hospital Association; the Minnesota Living Will Coalition; State Representative David Bishop for his years of persistence in pursuing passage of the Minnesota legislation; and Minnesota Senator Ember Reichgott, who assisted in its passage. And most of all, those many people whose names I do not know who shared their questions and comments, their life experiences and insights, during the many educational programs on advance directives that I was privileged to teach.

The contributions of the authors of the Patient Self-Determination Act of 1990, Senator John Danforth of Missouri and Senator Daniel Patrick Moynihan of New York, will be acknowledged and appreciated for years to come. Their foresight and wisdom have made it possible for advance directives to be recognized as an integral part of the plan of care for people who can no longer participate in decisions about their care.

E. J. VA.

CONTENTS

CHAPTER 1

THE VALUE
OF AN ADVANCE DIRECTIVE

Modern medical care is an impressive body of knowledge, skill, dedication, and technology. It can prevent many of the diseases that killed our ancestors; it can cure or control chronic diseases; it can delay death for days, weeks, even years. We rely on the skills of doctors, nurses, and an increasing number and variety of ancillary medical care professionals to keep us active and comfortable. Death and disability are strangers; we avert our eyes when they approach us and our loved ones. But all of us will encounter at least one of these intruders, death, at some point. It is prudent to be prepared, both for our own sakes and for the sakes of our loved ones.

THE CASE OF MRS. A

One family's dilemma comes to mind as an example of the anguish that accompanies a particularly difficult terminal condition. Several years ago a chaplain in a nursing home phoned me for advice. A resident in the home (we'll call her Mrs. A) was 91 years old and had been in a *persistent vegetative state* (PVS) for several years. In PVS, all function of the upper part of the brain has been lost. This means that a person is no longer able to control conscious actions such as thinking, speaking, and eating; the person is permanently unconscious, although not in a coma. The eyes still open and close; there are sleep and wake cycles; there can be repetitive, involuntary movements of arms and legs. Breathing, heartbeat, and certain other body processes continue, because the lower part of the brain, the brain stem, still functions. (If the entire brain ceases to function, the person is brain dead, which is the same as being dead, except that the body is on a respirator, which mechanically keeps the body breathing and the heart beating. This is a factor in organ donation, as discussed in Chapter 4.)

In Mrs. A's case, the PVS was due to numerous strokes that she'd had over the years. She was not able to talk or to recognize her family. She lay curled up in bed, fed through a tube that had been surgically placed into her stomach—a gastrostomy tube. She was given good nursing care and seemed comfortable. (In PVS, a person does not feel pain because of the deterioration of the part of the brain where pain is consciously experienced.) Jane, Mrs. A's daughter, was a devout person with strong religious beliefs and, after much prayer and many talks with her priest, came to the conclusion that what was being done for and to her mother was not right. She visited her mother every day, remembering her as the busy, friendly, deeply religious woman she had been. Jane felt that if her mother were able to decide, she would not want to be kept alive in her present condition but would want to be released to the next life. So Jane got up her courage and asked the doctor who was caring for her mother to stop the tube feeding and let her mother die in peace.

The doctor said, "That would be both immoral and illegal. You have no right to ask me to do such a thing." This made Jane feel terribly guilty, especially since one of her two daughters, the one who lived in another state, had accused her, over the telephone, of "wanting to kill Grandma." (Jane's other daughter, who lived in the same city and visited her grandmother occasionally, agreed with her mother's decision to request that Mrs. A be allowed to die.) Jane then talked with the nursing home administrator, who said that only the doctor could order the tube feeding stopped. The administrator did say, "You have the right to take your mother home if you are not satisfied with the doctor's decision." Later, the administrator asked the chaplain to talk with Jane, who by this time was feeling so confused, guilty, and overwhelmed that she did not want to press the issue any further.

The chaplain was deeply troubled by the way Jane's request had been handled and wanted both to assist Jane and to be prepared for similar cases in the future. The chaplain asked about policies, procedures, and other methods for addressing ethical dilemmas such as this. I shared policies of other nursing homes with her and, in a later conversation, learned that this nursing home was setting up an ethics committee to assist staff and residents and their families.

What can we learn from this troubling case? It illustrates a number of issues: the importance of communication; the rights of patients and families and the responsibility of caregivers to help them exercise those rights; and the misconceptions and misunderstandings that a few health care providers have about ethics and the law.

Mrs. A's physician was mistaken when he said that withdrawing the feeding tube was against the law. In his state, Minnesota, there is no law prohibiting withdrawing or withholding artificially administered nutrition and hydration (tube feeding). Minnesota's living will law specifically states that people should state their preferences regarding tube feeding or give the health care proxy authority to make such decisions. If such instructions are not given, feeding tube decisions are to be made according to "reasonable medical practice." So the doctor was wrong about Jane's request being illegal. When he called her request immoral, he was expressing his own opinion as to the right course of action. Medically, there was no question that she would die if the feedings were stopped; he may have believed that stopping the feeding was morally wrong. He was entitled to his belief, but he should have told Jane that this was his personal belief and offered to withdraw as her mother's physician.

What if Mrs. A's doctor or the nursing home administrator had said to her daughter, "Your mother has not made out a living will, so we cannot assume that she would want to have the tube feeding stopped." Most state living will laws, including Minnesota's, have a *no presumption* clause. Missouri's Life Support Declarations Act, for example, states, "This act shall create no presumption concerning the intention of an individual who has not executed a declaration to consent to the use or withholding of medical procedures." The Oklahoma Natural Death Act has a similar clause: "The failure of a qualified patient to execute a directive...shall create no presumption as to the patient's wishes regarding life-sustaining procedures." The term *qualified patient,* which is used in a number of state living will laws, refers to someone who has executed a directive and who has been determined by one or more physicians to have a terminal condition; usually the laws that contain this clause require that terminal condition be certified in writing.

Communication is the most important factor, however, and it is within our control. This means talking about death and dying with our family, our doctors, and other health care providers. We will discuss this at length in Chapter 3, but first we will address some issues and concerns relating to advance directives.

EUTHANASIA

Euthanasia is a topic that generates intense emotion as well as thoughtful reflection. Euthanasia is a deliberate act to cause death. The motivation for the act may be similar to that of most people who prepare advance directives: to reduce unnecessary pain and suffering and allow the person to die as quickly and as peacefully as possible. The difference is that the focus of an advance directive is medical treatment—how one wants it used or not used. It is a statement that one wishes to be *allowed* to die, not to be *caused* to die.

In spite of this difference, some people still believe that it is euthanasia to withhold or withdraw life-sustaining treatment, because without such treatment a person will die. This has given rise to the idea that to withhold life-sustaining treatment is *passive euthanasia,* while withdrawing it is *active euthanasia.* Added to this is the mistaken belief that withdrawing treatment is illegal. As a result, treatment sometimes is not begun because no one wants to face the decision to withdraw it, should it not prove beneficial to the patient. Common sense says that the decision makers would be better able to make an informed decision if treatment had been started with the understanding that it would be discontinued if there were no benefit.

I have written in my living will, "If, when I am diagnosed to have a terminal condition, my health care providers wish to try some form of treatment which they believe may provide relief, they may try it for a limited period of time for the purpose of determining if it is beneficial. If it does not benefit me within a reasonably short period of time, then they are to stop treatment." The purpose of this statement is twofold: to acknowledge respect for my doctor's judgment about treatments that might benefit me and to give specific permission to withdraw if there is no benefit.

Another way in which euthanasia might arise in the context of an advance directive is if a person requests assistance in dying, such as help in committing suicide or asking a doctor for a lethal injection. If this were written in a living will, the directive probably would not be accepted, that is, would not be placed in the medical record. Most state living will laws contain a clause similar to Arizona's: "Nothing in this Act is intended to condone, authorize, or approve mercy killing or to permit any affirmative or deliberate act or omission to end life other than to permit a person to select the natural process of dying as provided in this act." Maryland's law further states, "The provisions...may not be construed to permit any affirmative or deliberate act or omission to end life other than to permit the withholding or withdrawing of life-sustaining procedures from a declarant in a terminal condition." Note that this clause does not make a distinction between withdrawing and withholding life-sustaining treatment. (References on euthanasia are provided in the Bibliography section of the Appendix for readers who are interested in the topic.)

CONCERNS ABOUT ADVANCE DIRECTIVES

You may ask, "Might not living wills lead to involuntary euthanasia?" or "Isn't there a danger that advance directives and withdrawing or withholding life-sustaining treatment will lead to depriving people of necessary treatment?" or "Might not living wills be required for old people or for disabled people to save money on medical care?" These are sometimes called *slippery slope* concerns because of the assumption that there will be an automatic progression from one point—in this case, enacting laws that recognize advance directives—to an unintended end point such as depriving people of necessary health care. These concerns have been raised many times, especially when state legislatures have been debating passage of living will laws. We have already discussed the differences between euthanasia and advance directives, so let's look at the other issues.

DEPRIVING PEOPLE OF NECESSARY TREATMENT

There are many people in our country who are not receiving needed medical treatment—not because they have living wills but because they do not have health insurance. Our country spends much more on health care, measured as dollars spent per person, than does any other industrialized country. Yet we do not measure up as well on indicators of health such as infant mortality and most chronic disease rates. Much of this high cost is wasteful—expensive malpractice insurance for physicians and other health care providers, for example, and repetitive and unnecessary diagnostic tests done merely to protect against malpractice charges. We also do more expensive procedures such as heart by-pass surgery and organ transplants, which may, or may not, add years to a person's life. If that person happens to be you or me or one of our loved ones, we feel it is worth the cost, especially if we do not have to pay for it directly. But eventually we will all have to pay, so it is worth taking time to think about some of these problems.

HEALTH INSURANCE

The question of universal access to health care is being debated in the Congress and in state legislatures. Access to health care is based primarily on whether a person has health insurance. About 35 million Americans, many of them families with children, do not have health insurance; many others do not have adequate insurance. For most people under age 65, health insurance is provided through their employment. (Medicare is a form of health insurance for people 65 and older. It is discussed in Chapter 7.) When people become unemployed, they lose this benefit and have to pay for health insurance themselves; if they become poor enough, they may qualify for Medicaid. State governments are trying to control Medicaid costs, however, so this is not an adequate substitute for private health insurance. The cost of health insurance is increasing and, for many people, the covered benefits are decreasing, so even people who are employed are paying more and receiving less. The inability to pay for health care, rather than the influence of advance directives, is the reason that some people do not receive necessary care.

WHAT IS NECESSARY CARE?

This is one of the most difficult questions of all, both for doctors and other health care providers and for patients and their families. A quick and easy answer is that it is any care that is needed to make a person well, able to function, or comfortable. If we think about it, however, wellness and function may have different meanings for each of us, so this definition is not sufficient.

Another way to think about necessary care is to ask, "What is reasonable medical practice?" The answer will differ among doctors and between doctors and patients and their families. A recent Minnesota case, which drew national attention, is a poignant example of the confusion surrounding this question.

The Case of Helga Wanglie

Mrs. Wanglie was an active woman until 1989, when, at age 85, she fell and broke her hip. She was hospitalized and then went to a nursing home. In January 1990, when she had severe difficulty breathing, an emergency ambulance was called, a tube was inserted into her throat, and she was placed on a respirator. She never recovered her ability to breathe without the respirator and was transferred to a chronic care hospital. A week later, she had a cardiac arrest (her heart stopped beating). She was resuscitated and transferred to the intensive care unit of an acute care hospital. She did not recover consciousness, and later, when the suggestion was made that life-sustaining treatment be withdrawn, her family transferred her back to the large medical center where she had been placed on the respirator five months earlier. After a while, she was diagnosed as being in a persistent vegetative state. She remained on a mechanical ventilator, received tube feedings, and was treated with antibiotics for recurring pneumonia. Her husband refused to consent to withdrawing life-support treatment or to transfer her to a nursing home. Her two children agreed with her husband.

Mrs. Wanglie had not prepared an advance directive. Her husband's refusal to stop treatment was based in part on the fact that she had "strong religious beliefs." The Court in its findings of fact, noted that Mrs. Wanglie was "a devout Lutheran," which does not necessarily mean that she would choose life-sustaining treatment. The American Lutheran Church (ALC) in 1977, the Evangelical Lutheran Church in America in 1982, and the Missouri Lutheran Church have all issued statements that, while supporting the sanctity of life and opposing euthanasia, are similar in intent to the statement in the ALC report: "We affirm that in many instances heroic and extraordinary means used to prolong suffering of both the dying person and the loved ones is unkind."[1] This is a reminder that most religious groups do not believe that treatment must be provided when it is unduly burdensome and that membership in a particular church denomination cannot be considered an indication of an individual's wishes regarding medical treatment. Mrs. Wanglie's family said that when they had talked about the meaning of life and death, especially following the illnesses and deaths of others, Mrs. Wanglie had not expressed any opinion about her wishes; she had never said that she did not want treatment. This, perhaps, was a more accurate basis for substituted judgment than was the Court's.

Mrs. Wanglie's doctors and nurses believed that it was wrong to continue to provide aggressive treatment in an acute care hospital when there would be no medical benefit to Mrs. Wanglie. The basis for this belief was that it was medically unreasonable and an inappropriate use of resources. The cost of her care was more than $400,000 at that point. (The total cost at the time of her death was more than $700,000.[2]) Her care was paid for by her husband's medical insurance and Medicare. Nursing home care, which the family refused, would have been less expensive. The hospital went to court, but not for a direct decision to stop treatment. Instead, her doctor decided to ask for appointment of a guardian to make the decision. The court ruled that Mr. Wanglie, although not her legally appointed guardian, was an appropriate proxy, that he was acting in his wife's best interest.[3] Mrs. Wanglie died a short time later—18 months after being placed on the respirator.

Saving Money: Setting Limits

My purpose in discussing the case of Mrs. Wanglie is to stimulate thought, not to suggest that the elderly have a responsibility to refuse life-sustaining treatment to save money for society. Such decisions must be made by the entire society, through public policy, after much discussion by people of all ages. Is it right to spend money on aggressive treatment of people who are terminally ill when so many people do not have access to basic health care because they do not have health insurance? This question is being debated throughout our country. (For many developing and undeveloped countries, the question is not when to *stop* medical treatment but how to *provide* basic health care, especially to children.) It is an important question for each of us, as members of society, to consider, but not necessarily as we prepare our advance directives.

A number of people have attempted to begin a public discussion of how to set limits and control health care costs. Two of the most publicized—and criticized—are former Governor Richard Lamm of Colorado and Daniel Callahan, director of the Hastings Center, a nationally recognized organization that focuses on ethical problems in medicine and related issues. They have suggested that elderly people have a responsibility to future generations and that this responsibility includes accepting limits on medical treatment, especially if such treatment serves no purpose other than to stave off death for a time. Callahan summarizes the problem as follows: "Our affluence and refusal to accept limits have led and allowed us to evade some deeper truths about the living of a good life and the place of aging and death in that life."[4] Steven Miles, a physician ethicist involved in Mrs. Wanglie's case, has suggested that the issue is one of stewardship, a careful use of resources, rather than rationing.[5]

The state of Oregon addressed the question of necessary care in an attempt to provide basic health care for all its citizens. The people of Oregon were involved for several years in public meetings to discuss the allocation of health care dollars, focusing on the relative benefit of different procedures. Preventive and primary care, including prenatal care and basic health care for families and children were ranked high, while "high-tech" procedures such as organ transplants got lower ratings. Converting these priorities into practice was difficult, however, and the Oregon State Legislature chose to begin by applying them through the Medicaid program. This meant that limits were imposed only on people who depended on Medicaid to pay for their health care—people who were poor or who were eligible for Medicaid because of disability. The federal government, which pays approximately half of the Medicaid program costs, refused to approve the Oregon plan, saying that it violated the Americans with Disabilities Act.

Access to necessary health care for all people is an important ethical issue, as is the wise use of health care dollars, but it is not directly related to advance directives. I believe that it is wrong to waste money on nonbeneficial medical treatment. I also believe that self-determination is important. Therefore, I view preparing an advance directive for medical treatment at the end of life as a responsible act to be undertaken after careful consideration of one's values and duties to God, to self, and to others; I do not view advance directives as a means of solving the problem of fair distribution of health care resources. (References are provided in the Bibliography section of the Appendix for people interested in reading more on this topic.)

ADVANCE DIRECTIVES ARE VOLUNTARY ACTS

This is the most important protection we have. Deciding to prepare an advance directive is an individual decision, made voluntarily and intended to guide those who must make medical treatment decisions at a time when the individual is unable to make them. These are usually end-of-life decisions, and directives usually state that the person does not want life-sustaining treatment, although a person can request that all treatment be given until the moment of death.

All state living will laws prohibit requiring someone to make a living will as a condition of receiving health care or health insurance. There are other safeguards in these laws: it is illegal to forge, change, or destroy another person's living will; the importance of reasonable medical practice is recognized; the declarant (patient) must be in a terminal condition for a directive to go into effect. Furthermore, a person can revoke (cancel) a directive at any time by notifying the doctor or other health care provider. In addition to these protections, the Patient Self-Determination Act forbids health care providers from discriminating against a patient on the basis of whether he or she has or has not made an advance directive.

YOUR RIGHT TO MAKE DECISIONS FOR YOURSELF

A basic fact that is sometimes overlooked—and underestimated—is that all the state laws emphasize that you have the right, the power, to make medical decisions for yourself as long as you are able to do so. These laws do not *give* you that right, as we will see in Chapter 2, but they *protect* it. We should not relinquish this power. When a person is sick, it can be difficult to make decisions, to be assertive. Sometimes, family members or health care providers try to "protect" a sick person from difficult decisions, or they underestimate the person's ability to make such decisions. Although living will and durable power of attorney for health care laws safeguard the right to self-determination, the right must be exercised. We must be prepared to make health care decisions for ourselves as long as we are able to do so. Preparation includes thinking about the final period of one's life, talking with doctor and family about one's wishes, and preparing a written advance directive in case one is unable to make decisions. Such inability sometimes, but not usually, comes with a terminal condition. A study done in California in 1988-1989 found that one reason that the living wills of seriously ill persons were not a major factor in the care given was that very few of the patients lost their ability to make decisions for themselves. There was no need to rely on a written advance directive.[6]

In addition to these assurances, the courts have said that there are four situations in which the State's interest is stronger than an individual's right to self-determination: preservation of life, prevention of suicide, protection of innocent third parties, and preservation of the integrity of the medical profession. Most courts, however, have said that the closer a person is to death, the less powerful these State interests are and the stronger the individual's right to self-determination is.

WHY A WRITTEN DIRECTIVE?

You may well wonder, as I have, why a written advance directive is necessary, why talking with family, doctor, friends, and others is not sufficient. Why is it necessary to prepare a legal document to die? It would not be *if* you could be sure

- that you would not lose the ability to make decisions for yourself.
- that your family would remember all that you had talked about and would not be overcome with guilt or uncertainty if they had to consent to withhold or withdraw life-sustaining treatment.
- that there would be agreement among all members of your family as to your wishes or the wisdom of them.
- that your doctor would remember your discussions and that this same doctor would be involved in your care at the time end-of-life medical decisions had to be made.
- that no one would raise the question of legal liability if life-sustaining treatment were withheld or withdrawn.
- that compassion and common sense would always prevail.

It is impossible to assure in advance that all these conditions will be met. A written directive will provide some assurance that your wishes will be honored, but an equally important purpose is to ease the burden for the decision makers by providing them with guidance and evidence of your wishes. A written document provides evidence of your concern.

WILL AN ADVANCE DIRECTIVE
REALLY MAKE A DIFFERENCE?

Advance directives are a relatively recent part of both health care and legal systems in this country; they are still regarded with skepticism by some. Earlier we described a California study that seemed to indicate that advance directives did not make a difference in the care or the cost of care for 200 patients in two hospitals. These were people who had life-threatening diseases, half of whom were asked if they wished to complete a living will; two thirds of them did so. (Only two of those who prepared living wills requested aggressive treatment.) The remaining patients were not offered the chance to complete a living will. The presence or absence of a living will did not seem to make a difference in the care given, the amount of time spent in the hospital, or the cost of care. One conclusion drawn was that a living will is not a satisfactory means of doctor-patient communication.[7] I agree but would remind doctors and patients alike that a living will can stimulate such communication and serve as a reminder that it occurred and that conclusions were reached. Moreover, time and energy must be available to encourage good communication. Time is a scarce commodity in today's health care system. The chances of this changing in the near future are slim, so a written document may be the best alternative, albeit a poor one.

Another conclusion drawn from this study was that the Patient Self-Determination Act "is doomed to fail."[8] I do not agree with this conclusion. For one thing, the study was conducted between 1987 and 1989, before the law was passed. The PSDA went into effect in December 1991 and, as with any new measure, will take time to be become part of medical and consumer practice. If more people complete advance directives and discuss them with their doctors and families in advance of a serious illness, such directives will be recognized as serious documents and given due consideration in developing a plan for care.

This study did not address the benefit of an advance directive as a means of preparing one's self and one's loved ones for the end of this life. Such spiritual and emotional benefits argue strongly in favor of advance directives. So do not be discouraged by those who say an advance directive will not make a difference. It will make a difference for you and your loved ones and for those who will provide your care.

We must recognize, however, that advance directives are not all-powerful. They are limited by law and practice, but they are based on ethical and legal principles that give them considerable power.

CHAPTER 2

THE ETHICAL AND LEGAL BASIS OF ADVANCE DIRECTIVES

Basic ethical principles underlie many, if not most, of our laws. Autonomy, or self-determination, is the principle that applies to advance directives. The corresponding legal concept is usually stated as the right to privacy, although the United States Supreme Court, in the Nancy Cruzan decision, cited an individual's right to liberty as the basis for the right to refuse life-sustaining treatment. Autonomy, privacy, and liberty reflect the value that our society places on the individual and its respect for individual self-determination. In medical practice, informed consent is the way in which self-determination is applied.

INFORMED CONSENT

Informed consent means that people must consent to medical treatment. Physicians and other health care providers have a responsibility to give a patient the information needed to decide whether to consent to or refuse treatment. The patient must be able to receive and understand the information, think about it, make a decision, and explain the reason for the decision. This introduces the idea of *competency,* which is a legal determination in situations such as guardianship.

Informed consent depends on both the manner and the amount of information given to the patient and the patient's ability or competency to understand and to act. Medical practice varies among physicians and hospitals as to when and for which procedures informed consent is sought or required. If you have ever been a patient in a hospital, you probably signed a general consent form upon admission. Later, if you had surgery or another procedure considered to be invasive, you may have been asked to sign a specific consent form. Definitions of invasive procedures vary, as do the policies and practices of health care providers.

A nurse attending a conference on patients' rights said that her hospital did not require patient consent to insert a nasogastric feeding tube (a tube inserted into the stomach through the nose). When I asked the reason for this practice, she replied that the hospital did not require specific consent to insert an intravenous (IV) tube and that the nasogastric tube was not considered more invasive than an IV tube. Both tubes are part of a medical treatment, however, and informed consent should be required for both. Most health care providers and their lawyers, as well as medical ethicists, agree that only in an emergency can treatment be given without consent of the patient or the patient's surrogate and that consent must be obtained as quickly as possible. This exception is based on the premise that in a life-threatening situation, most people would want treatment; therefore, consent is implied. It's when we attempt to apply some of the practices of acute or emergency medicine to end-of-life medical treatment decisions that we can be faced with ethical dilemmas and legal conflicts. Although advance directives are not a magic solution to problems of informed consent, they can provide guidance to the decision makers. This means that it is important to be as specific as you can be in writing your directive and to give careful thought to your choice of a surrogate decision maker.

SURROGATE DECISION MAKER

When a patient is considered incapable of making a decision, of exercising informed consent, law and practice regarding surrogate (proxy) decision makers vary. Some states have specific laws related to proxy decision makers; others provide for durable power of attorney for health care; and still others have a provision for naming a proxy in a living will.

Medical practice has long been that those closest to the patient are asked to decide. Family members are considered appropriate surrogates because they know the person well and are most able to exercise *substituted judgment*—to decide as the patient would have decided. For an older patient, the surrogate typically is, in the following order: the spouse, adult children, brothers or sisters, nieces or nephews, or relatives through marriage. For children, parents usually are the decision makers, because children are not legally competent under state laws to give informed consent; they are not considered to have had the experience nor acquired the wisdom to exercise informed consent.

THE COURTS AS MEDICAL DECISION MAKERS

Beginning in the 1970's, the courts became more involved in medical decisions, especially in decisions involving withdrawing life-sustaining treatment. Health care providers and their legal counselors turned to the courts for guidance because of the lack of medical, ethical, legal, and political consensus about the appropriate use of medical knowledge and technology. One result of the increased involvement of the courts was an increased interest in and legislation governing advance directives, based on the principle of self-determination and the right to privacy.

Direct court intervention in cases involving forgoing life-sustaining treatment may be decreasing. Recent guidelines issued by a group of nationally recognized experts in law, medicine, and medical ethics recommend that most such decisions be made by the individuals involved at the bedside and that courts not become involved in life-sustaining medical treatment decisions unless there is genuine disagreement as to the patient's wishes or competency or the appropriate surrogate, or if a decision is not in accordance with state law. These guidelines affirm the principle that competent people have the right to make their own decisions about life-sustaining medical treatment, and they encourage the use of advance directives.[1]

GUARDIANSHIP

If you are considering advance planning for medical treatment or financial affairs, you should have a basic understanding of guardianship, a type of court involvement in decision making.[2] Guardianship has received a great deal of attention in recent years, due in part to increased awareness of neglect and abuse of elderly people and the resulting development of adult protection services. In addition, demographic factors such as longer life and increased family mobility contribute to the number of people without family or others to serve as surrogates to help them manage their affairs and make decisions.

Guardianship involves three parties: a person *(ward* or *conservatee)* who has been determined to be incompetent to exercise self-determination; a second party *(guardian* or *conservator*—it may be a corporation) appointed to be the surrogate decision maker for the first person; and a judge, usually in a probate court, whose legal responsibility is to determine that the first person is not competent to exercise self-determination and that the second party will make decisions that will be in the first person's best interest. A petition may be entered by the first person, but this is usually done by a second party—a relative, an adult protection agency, or someone else concerned about the person's apparent lack of ability to manage. If the judge determines that the person is unable to exercise self-determination in a particular area of competency such as financial management or personal care, or both, decision making is transferred to the second party, and the ward loses a number of rights, depending upon the petition and the court's determination. The court has a continuing responsibility to monitor each guardianship case to assure that the ward continues to need a surrogate decision maker and that the guardian is making decisions that are in the ward's best interest. Unfortunately, courts are busy and frequently under-staffed, so there is insufficient oversight, and people may be denied basic rights or even suffer harm within a system intended to protect them.

Guardianship, as it applies to medical decision making, raises the issue of harm and the related term, *best interest.* The guardian, who is the person required to exercise informed consent, has a legal responsibility to act in the ward's best interest. In the legal sense, best interest means "acting as a reasonable person would act under similar circumstances." For some guardians, this means using substituted judgment—trying to determine their ward's wishes and deciding as the ward would have decided. Other guardians may be guided by their own judgment and feelings and make a treatment decision that might be different from, even contrary to, the ward's, especially if the decision involves forgoing life-sustaining treatment. Or the guardian may misunderstand or be misinformed about the law relating to medical decisions. For this reason, as well as the more basic deprivation of the right to self-determination, guardianship for medical decision purposes should be used only when and if less restrictive alternatives are unavailable.

Two medical treatment decisions, artificially administered nutrition and hydration (tube feeding) and cardiopulmonary resuscitation (CPR), are particularly difficult for guardians. They are difficult ones for all surrogate decision makers but especially for guardians, seemingly because of their role as court-appointed surrogates. A number of guardians and administrators of guardianship programs have told me that their lawyers advise them never to consent to withdrawing a feeding tube or to refuse consent to have one inserted, "because you could be legally liable." The same advice is given for consent to a No CPR order. Guardians are advised to go back to court for approval of these medical decisions. There is no evidence to support this legal advice, but misunderstanding of the law and medical practice continues to support the role of the courts in medical decision making.

Advance planning, including preparing an advance directive and naming a proxy decision maker, provides some assurance against guardianship solely for medical decisions in most situations. Should guardianship become necessary, the court is likely to appoint the person you select as proxy to act as your guardian, unless there is substantial evidence that your selected proxy is not an appropriate surrogate. If a stranger were appointed, a written directive would guide the guardian and the doctors and nurses to make the medical decisions you would have made.

PATIENTS' BILL OF RIGHTS

Most states have some form of a bill of rights for hospital patients and nursing home residents. There is also a federal Nursing Home Residents' Bill of Rights. These rights are usually posted in hospital and nursing home lobbies or other public areas and are given to patients and residents upon admission. The rights typically include the following:

- The right to considerate and respectful care.
- The right to have a person whom you choose participate in planning for your care and treatment.
- The right to information about your diagnosis, treatment and prognosis (probable outcome), and all other information needed to exercise informed consent, which includes the right to refuse treatment.
- The right to privacy. This means that your medical records are confidential. You have the right to review your medical record, as does your proxy. (Information from your medical record is made available to payors of health insurance via a release, which you will be asked to sign when you enter a hospital or nursing home.)
- The right to examine your hospital or nursing home bills and to have them explained to you.

The patients' bill of rights can be helpful when preparing an advance directive; you may want to obtain a copy from your local hospital or nursing home.

In addition to the state laws related to patients' rights, the American Hospital Association has issued a policy statement entitled, "A Patient's Bill of Rights," which is included in the Appendix of this book. I recommend that you read it before starting the next part of the book, the "nuts and bolts" section. Not only does it summarize some of the issues we've discussed so far but it should provide an understanding of the duties of health care providers. It also emphasizes the importance of collaborative decision making, which provides the best assurance that your advance directive will be followed.

The best of laws, policies, and intentions, however, do not assure patient self-determination. Patients may be too ill to understand or exercise such rights, especially if the decision involves forgoing life-sustaining treatment. Family members may be distraught, exhausted, or absent. There may be many doctors involved in a complicated medical situation, and neither patient nor family may be sure who is in charge. There are resources within a hospital or nursing home to which patients and families can turn for help, especially if they are not comfortable with or able to talk with the physician or if there is disagreement about the treatment. Let's return to Mrs. A's case.

Mrs. A had not prepared a directive, but she had other rights, which under usual medical practice, would have included having her daughter serve as her surrogate decision maker. She had a right to change physicians. The nursing home administrator should have given Jane this information and could have offered to assist her in finding a physician who would honor her request. Such assistance is required under the living will laws of many states. Some hospitals and nursing homes also have policies regarding a patient's right to change physicians and the institution's responsibility to assist in the change.

How does a patient or a patient's family find out about these laws and policies or about their right to informed consent? And who educates health care providers about the ethical principles, laws, and standards of practice? Many hospitals and an increasing number of nursing homes have biomedical ethics committees whose purpose is to educate, develop policies, and review individual cases related to ethical issues. Had an ethics committee reviewed Mrs. A's case, it would have advised the concerned parties regarding the ethical and legal issues involved and, perhaps, recommended a course of action.

In addition to ethics committees, chaplains and social workers are available in most hospitals and nursing homes to advise and advocate in such situations. In hospitals, patient representatives are available to provide assistance. The responsibility still rests with the patient and family, however, to exercise their rights.

MEDICAL MALPRACTICE SUITS

Mrs. A's physician was not a bad person, nor was the nursing home administrator. They may have been misinformed about some of the ethical principles and laws surrounding the withdrawal of life-sustaining treatment, but they undoubtedly felt they were doing what was right. Unfortunately, "right" often translates to "avoiding risk" in the legalistic, litigious environment of modern health care. Many health care providers are afraid of being sued if they do *not* provide life-sustaining treatment, regardless of patient or family consent. Fear of being sued is real. Physicians I know who have been sued, even though the suits were unsuccessful, say it is one of the worst experiences a person can have. Although an understanding of patients' rights is important for both patients and health care providers, trust is the most important factor in ensuring that one's wishes for treatment will be honored at the end of life. It also is a factor in reducing the fear of a malpractice suit. Trust is built through communication, respect, and familiarity. Getting to know one's doctor can be difficult in these days of specialized medicine, managed care, and cost controls. It is well worth the effort, however, to establish a relationship in which collaborative decision making involving doctor, patient, and family can take place. We'll offer some suggestions in the following chapters.

CHAPTER 3

GETTING STARTED

Getting started is often the most difficult part of any task. Perhaps you, like many others, have obtained a living will form but have not completed it, so it lies in a desk drawer, a silent reminder of a task undone. My intent in this chapter is to guide you through an apparently complicated process that can be made much simpler if taken one step at a time.

Step One: Finding Out about Your State's Law

The first step is to find out about your own state's law or laws pertaining to advance directives. Because of the federal Patient Self-Determination Act (PSDA), you will be given some information about the law if you enter a hospital or nursing home, begin home health or hospice care, or enroll in an HMO. This information may not provide the level of detail that you will need, nor is that the time to begin thinking about an advance directive. You should prepare your directive before you are hospitalized or enter a nursing home because of a chronic or terminal illness; it takes time to write a thoughtful directive.

There are two types of laws about advance directives. One type provides for a written directive—called a living will, a declaration, a directive, or a terminal care document, depending upon the state in which you live. These directives go into effect only when a doctor determines that you have a terminal condition (some states require two doctors to certify in writing that you have a terminal condition).

The second type of law provides for appointing a health care proxy. Most of these are called durable power of attorney for health care (DPAHC) laws, although New York's is called a Health Care Proxy Appointment, and Michigan's is a Designation of Patient Advocate for Health Care. Some living will laws have a provision for appointing a health care proxy. These laws make it possible for you to appoint, in writing, someone to make health care decisions for you when you cannot do so. Under a DPAHC, the surrogate decision maker is usually called an *agent* or an *attorney-in-fact,* although the person does not have to be a lawyer; usually it's a family member or trusted friend. Most DPAHC laws do not require that a person be terminally ill before the agent can make decisions. Ohio's DPAHC law is an exception; it prohibits the attorney-in-fact from refusing or withdrawing consent for life-sustaining treatment, comfort care, or nutrition or hydration unless death is imminent. In Ohio, the attorney-in-fact cannot refuse life-sustaining treatment for a pregnant woman if it would terminate the pregnancy, unless the treatment or the pregnancy would pose a substantial risk to the woman's life or the fetus is dead. (Many state living will laws place a prohibition on implementing a directive to forgo life-sustaining treatment for a pregnant woman.) In Texas, the agent may not consent to placement in a mental institution or to electric shock treatment, psychosurgery, or abortion. A few other state DPAHC laws also place some restrictions on the proxy.

Your first step, therefore, is to find out about your state's laws on advance directives and the requirements and restrictions they contain. The restrictions usually apply to one or more of the following:

- The form to use.
- When the directive goes into effect.
- Witnesses.
- Withholding or withdrawing tube feeding.
- Pregnancy.

You can find out about your state's law on advance directives from the following sources (you may have to try more than one):

- Hospital, nursing home, or hospice.
- Public health or home nursing agency.
- Your health maintenance organization (HMO).
- Your doctor.
- Your lawyer.
- A community library.
- Senior citizens' groups.
- State hospital association. (See Resource section.)
- State medical association. (See Resource section.)

- State bar association. (See Resource section.)
- Choice in Dying Association. (See Resource section.)

When requesting information, you should ask these questions:

1. Do I have to have a special form for my living will? If the answer is yes, ask where you can get the form and how much it costs. The charge is usually nominal—no more than $5 for a form, slightly more if a packet of instructions is included. Some office supply and bookstores sell copies of the forms but usually do not include information about the law. Beware of sales pitches in mail order catalogs, even though they advertise forms that are "Good in all 50 states!" Each state is different. A generic form that you can use, if your state does not require a specific one, can be obtained from Choice in Dying; the address is included in the Resource section of the Appendix. It is not necessary to write your directive on a form, even in those states that require directives to conform substantially to the wording in the law, but the form will give you a guide to follow. You can attach additional instructions to a form.

2. Can I appoint a health care proxy in my living will? Is there a Durable Power of Attorney for Health Care law? Are there restrictions on who can be a proxy or agent? We will discuss health care proxies, including DPAHC, in Chapters 5 and 6, so it is essential that you know if your state provides for either, both, or neither and if there are any restrictions as to who can serve. Some states, for example, do not permit the treating physician or other health care provider to be an agent. In some, the designation of a spouse as the proxy is revoked upon divorce.

3. When will my directive go into effect? When does it become operational? The reason for asking it both ways is that some state laws say that the directive becomes effective or operative when it is delivered to the physician or other health care provider, when it becomes part of your medical record. Living will laws, however, require people to be in a terminal condition before the directive actually goes into effect. (DPAHC laws, with the exception of Ohio's, do not have the terminal condition requirement.) Terminal condition is defined differently in each state. In New Hampshire, for example, a terminal condition is "an incurable condition caused by injury, disease, or illness which is such that death is imminent and the application of life-sustaining measures would, within the

reasonable medical judgment of the attending physician and a consulting physician, only postpone the moment of death." Maine defines it as "an incurable or irreversible condition that, without the administration of life-sustaining procedures, will, in the opinion of the attending physician, result in death within a short time." In Minnesota, it's "an incurable or irreversible condition for which the administration of life-sustaining procedures will serve only to prolong the dying process." Although Arkansas's definition of terminal condition is similar to Maine's, Arkansas's law, which is called the Rights of the Terminally Ill and Permanently Unconscious Act, applies also to people who have a "lasting condition, indefinitely without change in which thought, feeling, sensations and awareness of self and environment are absent." It is essential, therefore, to find out how terminal condition is defined in your state so that you know when your directive becomes effective.

In addition to the terminal condition requirement, many state living will laws prohibit withdrawing life-supporting treatment from a terminally ill pregnant woman if there is a possibility that the fetus can be born alive. Although this provision would affect very few of the people who prepare advance directives, if you are a woman of child-bearing age, you should be aware of this restriction.

4. Are there any kinds of medical treatment that I cannot refuse under the living will law? If the answer is yes, ask which ones.

5. Can I refuse artificially administered nutrition and hydration (tube feeding) if I so choose? It's important to ask this question in addition to Question 4, because some state laws define tube feeding as comfort care, which must always be provided, rather than as life-sustaining treatment. Some states require that death be imminent before tube feeding can be withheld or withdrawn. In these states, even if you wrote, "I do not want life-sustaining treatment," you would not be refusing tube feeding. North Dakota's law, for example, contains two forms, called "Declaration to Physicians." Declaration Form A is for people who do not want life-prolonging treatment; Declaration Form B is for those who want life-prolonging treatment. What Form A does not say is that, under North Dakota's Natural Death Act, tube feeding is not defined as part of life-prolonging treatment; people are not permitted to refuse tube feeding unless it results in pain or harm. If you did not want tube feeding, neither form would reflect your wishes. North Dakota

residents are not required to use these forms, however. North Dakota also has a DPAHC law, which does not place restrictions on tube feeding or other treatment decisions, nor is it limited to a terminal condition. North Dakota residents who do not want tube feeding, would be well-advised to complete a directive such as the one shown in Chapter 6 or the Living Will in the Appendix and to appoint a proxy through the DPAHC.

6. Who can witness my directive? Most states place some restrictions on witnesses. As a rule, the proxy cannot be a witness, nor can someone who would benefit from the declarant's estate. Therefore, do not have a family member sign as a witness. In some states, health care providers, including hospital and nursing home employees, cannot witness a directive; in some, a notary public can be used instead of two witnesses; others require two witnesses and a notary. In some states, if the declarant is in a nursing home, a representative of the state human services or ombudsman's office must be one of the witnesses.

    The purpose of having the witnesses or notary is to assure that the directive was signed by the declarant and signed voluntarily. In a few states, the witnesses also testify that the declarant is of "sound mind," although this is an opinion, not a professional determination of competency.

7. How often must I renew my directive? Most states do not require renewal; the directive remains effective until and unless you revoke it. A few states do require that either the living will or the DPAHC, or both, be rewritten or renewed periodically. California, for example, requires the written directive to physicians to be renewed every five years, the DPAHC every seven. In Oregon, a DPAHC appointment is effective for seven years unless the principal becomes unable to make health care decisions during that time, in which case it continues in effect until the principal regains that ability or dies.

8. How can I revoke (cancel) my directive? Under all state laws, a directive can be revoked at any time, but only by the declarant or someone acting for the declarant. Most of the laws state that the declaration can be revoked "regardless of the declarant's mental competency"; some include physical competency. Most laws permit either written or oral revocation. The revocation must be given to the physician or other health care provider, who must record it in the medical record. DPAHC laws are typically less specific about

revocation than living will laws, so be sure to find out how you can revoke appointment of your agent.

Be sure to ask if the information you are given is current—if it includes all amendments—because state legislatures change and add to these laws regularly.

Step Two: Deciding on the Type of Directive

The best way to ensure that your treatment wishes will be honored is to both make out a living will and appoint a proxy decision maker. By doing so, you are providing instructions that will be in your medical record and in your proxy's hands, and you will be picking someone you know and trust to make decisions for you. You can appoint a proxy in a living will or through a durable power of attorney for health care; I recommend doing both.

The advantage of the DPAHC is that your agent (proxy) will be able to make decisions for you, especially to refuse life-sustaining treatment, if that is your wish, before you are determined to be in a terminal condition. Most agents under a DPAHC can begin to make decisions as soon as the principal is no longer able to do so, which may be before he or she is determined to be in a terminal condition as defined in a particular state's law. In states where a living will does not go into effect until death is "imminent" or expected to occur "within a short time," your proxy under a living will might not be able to refuse any treatment, even if you had so instructed. It could be even more difficult to stop any life-sustaining treatment that had been started. Therefore, if you do not want treatment started or continued after the point at which you have decided that it's time to die, but the law says you are not in a terminal condition, you would be better served by a DPAHC agreement. Again, remember that as long as you are able to make your own decisions, you have the right to do so.

The type of treatment that can be refused in a living will—tube feeding, in particular—is also restricted in a number of states. Such restrictions are especially important considerations in conditions such as Alzheimer's and other forms of dementia, in persistent vegetative state and other forms of permanent unconsciousness, in chronic heart and other circulatory diseases, and in chronic respiratory and kidney diseases. Most DPAHC laws do not place restrictions on the type of treatment decisions the agent can make.

My advice is that if your state's living will law provides for appointing a proxy in the living will, do so. If your state has a durable power of attorney for health care law, complete that document as well. Be sure to appoint the same person in both documents, however, to avoid confusion when decisions must be made for you. (We'll address choosing a proxy in Chapter 5.)

If your state doesn't have a DPAHC law, you can use a general durable power of attorney (DPA) agreement, which all states have. You can probably find the form at an office supply store or obtain one from a lawyer. The DPA laws apply primarily to financial affairs, but in the absence of a DPAHC law, they can be used to appoint a health care proxy. Although there is a difference of opinion as to the legality of the general DPA for health care decisions, many health care providers will accept it. There have not been any court decisions or other legal opinions prohibiting its use; there have been decisions and opinions in some states that recognize and permit use of the DPA for health care decisions. There are not as many protections built into the general DPA laws, however, so it's especially important that you name someone you know and trust as your health care proxy.

What if your state is one of the few that doesn't have a living will law? It's still important to make a written directive and to state your wishes as specifically as possible. Your doctor, guided by reasonable medical practice and the principle of informed consent, should still follow your instructions. In the unfortunate situation in which either you or your family must go to court or the health care providers request a court decision, the document will provide written evidence of your wishes.

If your state has restrictions on when or what kinds of treatment you or your proxy can refuse and you do not want such treatment under any circumstances, write your wishes in your directive even if they conflict with the law. Some courts have ruled that state law cannot override a person's constitutional rights.

The Case of Estelle Browning

In Florida in 1986, Estelle Browning, who was 86 years old, had a severe stroke. She lost her ability to swallow, and a feeding tube was inserted into her stomach. She was eventually diagnosed as being in a persistent vegetative state, and after two years, her guardian, a second cousin, filed a petition with the court to have the tube feeding stopped. Mrs. Browning had prepared a living will in 1980 and re-executed it in 1985 because one of the witnesses to her first directive had died. She stated that she did not want treatment, including tube feeding, if she were in a terminal condition. Florida's law defines a terminal condition as one in which death is imminent. The lower court ruled that the feeding tube could not be withdrawn, that death was not imminent because, with tube feeding, she could live indefinitely.

In 1990, the Florida Supreme Court overturned the lower court's decision. It held that Mrs. Browning's condition was terminal, and death was imminent because she would die shortly if the treatment (tube feeding) were stopped. The Court said that Mrs. Browning had a fundamental right to self-determination; that the right extends to all health care decisions and to all types of treatment; that if a person has left instructions regarding life-sustaining treatment, the surrogate must make the choice that the patient would have made. Furthermore, not only legal guardians, but other proxies may exercise that right for an incompetent patient.[1]

Mrs. Browning died before the Florida Supreme Court issued its decision, so she did not benefit directly from it. Her case does, however, benefit those of us who wish to exercise our right to self-determination. It demonstrates the value and power of an advance directive. As a result of the Court's decision, this clause was added to Florida's living will form: "In addition, whether or not my death is imminent, I direct that if I have a terminal condition or am irreversibly unconscious, nutrition and hydration (food and water) not be provided by tubing or intravenously." The requirement of terminal condition is retained in the remainder of the law, however. This means that the attending physician must determine that there can be no recovery and death is imminent. It is not clear how this distinction between tube feeding and other types of treatment might affect treatment decisions for people who are not in a terminal condition as defined by Florida law.

Another lesson provided by the Browning decision is that a directive must provide "clear and convincing evidence" of the person's wishes. The United States Supreme Court, in the Nancy Cruzan decision, also used "clear and convincing evidence" as the standard. This, then, is the challenge: to put your thoughts into writing in a manner that will be clear and convincing.

Step Three: Thinking about Disability, Death, and Dying

This step is one of the most difficult in the preparation of an advance directive. It is essential, however, in making a meaningful directive. It is not an easy task, nor should it be.

At this point, you have gathered information about your state's law or laws and have obtained copies of the necessary forms. Now comes the hard part! You have to think about the end of your own life. This means taking time to think about how *you* regard death, disability, and dependency—how you view yourself, including your relationship to God and to other people.

For some, religious beliefs will be the basis for their instructions. I recall one woman who said, at a meeting where I was trying to explain Minnesota's proposed living will law, "My religion teaches me that suffering is a part of dying, that it's part of God's will. I suppose if this law is passed they won't let me suffer!" I explained that it would be prudent for her to make out a living will, even if the law were not passed. She should state, in writing, that she did not want so much pain-killing medication or sedative that she would not be able to feel or think when she faced death.

As I ponder the end of my life, I remember bits and pieces, words from books and from other people, that have special meaning for me. You will have your own sources of inspiration—your beliefs and your values. Think about them as they apply to this last part of your life. Some books that I have found especially helpful are listed in the Bibliography section of the Appendix.

A scene from a favorite book of my childhood comes to mind: Peter Pan, when he was standing on the rock and the water was rising around him, said, "To die will be an awfully big adventure!" (I think of it as awe-fully.) I find much inspiration in a book written by a physician, Arnold Beisser, who, at age 25, contracted polio and was permanently paralyzed from the neck down. He has continued to practice medicine and live life fully for 40 more years. The following passage is especially meaningful to me:

> True reverence for life includes all life, not just that of any single individual. All life must share the common fate on earth of death. If we can reserve at least a part of who we are for the whole of life, individual death is not so overwhelming.[2]

In the introduction to his book, Dr. Beisser writes, "... I realize I must make peace with death, if I am to live my life with grace." Preparing an advance directive adds to the peace of mind that makes it possible to live more fully.

We often think or say, "I want a natural death," meaning a peaceful death, free of machines and tubes, perhaps at home with family gathered round as we slip quietly away. This is an ideal that is difficult to achieve. Statistics show that 80 percent of the deaths in this country occur in either a hospital or a nursing home. And, although we hear about cases in which people are not allowed to die in a hospital or nursing home—perhaps because their families went to court—these are the exceptions. Death can occur peacefully in any setting, although hospice care perhaps most closely approximates what most people think of as a "natural" death. It's important, therefore, to state your wishes not only about specific treatments but about the type of care you want. (See Chapter 4.)

Think, as you prepare to write your advance directive, "What do my beliefs and feelings mean when applied to medical treatment?" To help in this task, the Values History, prepared by the Center for Health Law and Ethics of the University of New Mexico, is included in the Resource section of the Appendix. I suggest you begin with Section II. If you decide to fill out the Values History form, make a copy for your proxy and others who may be involved in carrying out your instructions. Keep the original with your advance directive. Ask your doctor to have it made part of your medical record when it becomes operational, that is, when the time comes to develop a plan for terminal care for you. It will add meaning to your directive and assist the decision makers.

After you've thought about your beliefs and values, think about any life and death medical experiences you may have had—experiences that threatened your life or the life of someone who was close to you. My first husband died suddenly in bed beside me of heart failure. He'd had an operation the year before to replace a heart valve damaged by rheumatic fever he had as a child. He said several times that he would never want to go through the surgery and recovery again, even though he was now able to work and live a relatively normal life. (This happened 25 years ago when heart surgery was relatively new.) He did not have a living will. We had never heard of such a thing at the time, although we had both signed anatomical gift donation forms, willing our bodies to a medical school for teaching purposes. At the time he died, there was no well-developed emergency medical system, no 911 to call. Would I have called one? I don't know. Looking back, based on experiences I have had since then, probably not. I know that he did not want to undergo surgery again, that he'd suffered pain and discomfort, that he still did not feel well. If he could have been resuscitated, he would probably have faced more surgery.

I now know, after reading many studies of the effectiveness of cardiopulmonary resuscitation (CPR), that, given his heart problems, even with CPR, the probability that he would recover would be low—probably less than 5 percent. I also know that the probability of permanent brain damage following CPR is also about 5 percent. On the other hand, my husband was a relatively young man of 47, the father of four children. At the time, there was—fortunately or unfortunately, depending on your point of view—no decision for me to make, but this experience and the deaths of elderly parents have shaped my beliefs. If I become chronically ill, I do not want CPR begun when my heart stops beating or my breathing stops.

Others may want CPR; they may want to take a chance on even low odds. I am reminded of a woman, who several years ago, when I was relating the low probability of successful resuscitation of people with chronic illness, said, "My husband had a heart attack when he was 78, and I called 911. The paramedics resuscitated him, and we had two good years together after that." This shows the importance of making your advance directive a statement of your wishes, based on your experiences and belief.

What are some things to think about as you begin to prepare your written directive? Here are some questions to ask yourself:

- What kind of serious conditions can I expect?
- What kind of treatments might be used for those conditions?
- What are the chances that treatment will benefit me?
- What do I mean by benefit?
- What would happen if treatment did not benefit me?
- What are the costs?
- What if I change my mind?

Chronic diseases can be treated, and people can be active for many years. Most progress to the point where treatment no longer controls the symptoms or keeps the person functioning as he or she once did—the benefits decrease. So we should focus on the resulting conditions, rather than the disease when preparing an advance directive.

At some point in the development of a chronic disease the disease will probably get to the point where treatment no longer controls it and the person faces increasingly severe symptoms and treatments. Or the condition will affect the person's mental ability because of strokes or Alzheimer's Disease or other damage to the brain. That is the point at which you should direct your thinking—the point when you believe that you will not benefit from further treatment. When that time arrives, the plan for your care should be based on your determination of benefit. (For more about care plans, see Chapter 5.)

Benefit means benefit to the declarant, the person who has made the advance directive. In my living will I state, "I do not want care and treatment provided because it makes someone else feel better. I want my loved ones and those who provide care to me to know that by letting me die, they are carrying out my wishes. They are not to feel guilty but are to remember how I lived." I thought about this for some time, trying to decide if I were being selfish, but then decided that it was my gift to my loved ones.

Let me share some of the recurring thoughts and questions I have gleaned from participants in the living will educational programs I've taught:

Is it enough to say that I want treatment stopped if I have a condition that makes it impossible for me to carry out my usual activities, care for myself, or one in which it is impossible to control my pain and suffering? This is a good statement of overall wishes and could be used to begin your the treatment part of your directive. It would not meet the restrictive definition of terminal condition required under the living will laws of many states. Under a DPAHC, your agent, in consultation with your doctor, would make the decision; this statement should be regarded as the basis of a plan for specific treatment decisions.

What if I write that I don't want treatment and then change my mind? I might decide that I am willing to put up with the restricted activity, pain, or discomfort because there are other benefits from the treatment. You can change your mind and revoke or revise your directive at any time. Also, as long as you are able to make treatment decisions, you can make them; you can consent or refuse to consent to treatment.

What if I'm not able to exercise informed consent, if, for example, I have advanced Alzheimer's disease and then get kidney disease and my doctor recommends kidney dialysis? What if I'm already on kidney dialysis; will they stop it? What if I get pneumonia; will they treat it? If you had stated that you did not want life-sustaining medical treatment—no additional treatment begun or existing treatment withdrawn—you would expect your doctor or your proxy to honor your instructions. If you lived in a state where the definition of terminal condition was narrow, however, where death had to be imminent or expected to occur within a very short time, the answer would be less certain. This is why the next step, talking about your thoughts and instructions, is so important.

What if I want treatment, want everything done to keep me alive? Will my wishes be honored? If you believe that you would want all available treatment for your condition begun and continued until death occurred, you have the right to say so; a directive is a statement of individual wishes. Although advance directives are usually used by people who do not want medical treatment that will only prolong dying, they may be used by those who do want treatment until they die. Your doctor is not obligated to provide treatment that is not considered to be reasonable medical practice, however. As we learned in the case of Helga Wanglie, reasonable medical practice may conflict with patient self-determination.

The question, "What are the costs"?, is closely related to the question, "What happens if treatment doesn't benefit me?" When a chronic disease, an infectious disease such as AIDS, or the injuries resulting from a severe accident progress to the point where people can no longer care for themselves, the costs can be astronomical.(This is not to say that beneficial treatment is not costly, as anyone who pays for drugs or other treatment well knows.) Treatment without benefit imposes additional emotional, physical, and financial costs on all who are involved, not just the patient. Why not say in a living will, "I don't want my money spent on medical care when treatment will no longer benefit me"? I ask this question when I speak on advance directives. The responses vary. Some people nod in agreement; others say, "You can't talk about money when life is involved." I then say, "But I'd rather have my money spent on someone else—educating my grandchildren or helping others. Is that wrong?" One of our children asked, "What if we'd like you around a bit longer regardless of how much it costs?" I reminded her of the statement in my living will that I did not want to be kept alive just to make someone else feel better.

I trust you can see how important both the thinking and the talking steps are to all involved in carrying out an advance directive and can understand why preparing a directive is time-consuming. It should be, which is why you should not wait until you are in the hospital or a nursing home to prepare one.

Remember Mrs. A, her daughter Jane, and Jane's two daughters? The one who lived in another state accused her of "wanting to kill Grandma." If Mrs. A had prepared an advance directive, the conflict might have been avoided. Or if Jane and both her daughters had thought and talked about what Mrs. A would have wanted, as did Helga Wanglie's family, perhaps Jane would have been spared some heartache. Talking with family and others is an essential step.

Step Four: Talking to Others about Your Wishes

After you've thought about your beliefs and your wishes concerning medical treatment, talk about them with your family and others who may be involved in caring for you. The purpose is twofold: to let them know that you are planning to prepare a directive and how you feel about care and treatment— especially life-sustaining treatment— and to get a feeling for their response. (After you have written your directive, you should talk with them again about your specific wishes.) It's not easy to begin this discussion. One reason for securing a copy of a form at the beginning of the process is that it can serve as the catalyst for talking with your family and others.

My second husband and I have eight children between us. The times when we are all gathered together are usually holidays, birthdays, or other special celebrations. We've been reluctant to bring up what some of them view as a difficult, even morbid, topic during these gatherings. For some families, such gatherings might be the most appropriate time to talk about this special family responsibility. We have each discussed our wishes with our children individually and in detail with the child each of us has asked to serve as proxy. Our next step will be to bring the families together to discuss both our advance directives for medical care and our living trust for financial affairs. (For more about the latter, see Chapter 7.)

If your family and the person you will be trusting to be your proxy (who probably will be a family member) are supportive of advance directives and of your feelings about the extent of treatment you wish to receive, you will be able to proceed more quickly to completing your directive. If any or all seem uncomfortable or resistant to the idea, you may need to provide them with more information and talk with them some more. If some member of your family is especially resistant or openly opposed either to advance directives or to your feelings about treatment, you have a potential problem. You would certainly not ask this person to serve as proxy, but you should try to determine the reason for his or her opposition. Perhaps you could ask the person to accompany you to meet with someone who is knowledgeable about advance directives and terminal care—perhaps a hospice nurse or social worker.

It would be helpful to talk with your doctor at this point to learn about her or his experiences with living wills and secure advice related to your state of health or illness. Bring a list of questions—those from Step Three (which are included in the check list in the Appendix) and any others that may have occurred to you. If you do not have an appointment scheduled, you might consider making one for this purpose. You may have to pay for such a visit out of your own pocket, however, as most health insurance will not reimburse for "educational visits." It could be well worth the cost.

Other people whose comments would be helpful at this point are a minister, priest, or rabbi; nurses, especially those who work in hospice or home health care, intensive care, or emergency rooms; and medical social workers. A lawyer might be able to give advice if he or she has had experience in health care. You do not need to have a lawyer prepare your directive, but there are some situations in which it would be prudent to have a lawyer involved. If, for example, you should decide to choose someone other than a family member to serve as your proxy or if you anticipate disagreement or conflict among family members, it might well be helpful to have a legal advocate aware of your wishes and available to see they are followed.

In addition to family, close friends can be helpful when preparing an advance directive. Many have personal experiences and insights to share. I know of three young women who, after each had thought about preparing a living will for many months, decided to get together to talk about their feelings and wishes. They found that sharing their beliefs and experiences helped them progress to the next step. They began writing their directives at that time, although each completed her own individually.

What about other groups or group meetings? Many hospitals, nursing homes, churches, and senior citizens' groups sponsor programs on how to prepare an advance directive. Before enrolling in such a program, ask about the qualifications of the speaker. Most of these programs are helpful, most of the speakers are prepared, and most of the questions and comments of other participants are useful. I have, however, heard tales of speakers who did not understand the state law or had not had experience in a health care setting. Do not prepare your directive in a group meeting; this should be done after you have had time to think and talk with family and others who will be involved in your care. And remember that you are the expert! Only you know what you want when you face the end of your life.

The next step will be writing your directive, but first we'll look at some of the medical treatments that you should think about before making decisions.

CHAPTER 4

MEDICAL TREATMENTS, THERAPIES, AND CARE

In Chapter 3, we discussed general beliefs and wishes about medical treatment in the last years of our lives. Now we will focus on some of the more typical treatments for which decisions may need to be made. It is impossible to anticipate all the illnesses that one could have or the treatments for them, and new treatments are being developed all the time. You are not expected to make an exhaustive disease and treatment list, but it is not sufficient merely to say, "I want ordinary but not extraordinary treatment." The intent of such a statement is that you want care necessary for comfort and other support, but you do not want medical treatment that postpones death; the focus is on the *effect* of the care and treatment on the person. What sometimes happens, however, is that decision makers—family as well as doctors—focus on the *treatment,* rather than its effect on the person.

The Declaration of Euthanasia, issued by the Vatican in 1980, addresses this issue well. (See Bibliography: Statements of Religious Groups.) It says that "due proportion" should be used when determining when medical treatment should or should not be given. Due proportion means weighing the benefit of a particular treatment against its burden on the person and the family; there should be a due proportion of benefit rather than undue burden. The Declaration further states that health care providers are not morally obligated to provide, nor individuals to consent to, treatment that is disproportionately (unduly) burdensome. Imposing excessive expense on family or community is cited in the Declaration as a burden.

The two treatments we will discuss in detail are cardiopulmonary resuscitation (CPR) and artificially administered nutrition and hydration (tube feeding). We will look briefly at some other treatments. The reason for discussing CPR and tube feeding in detail is that they are treatments about which many decision makers will have to decide. They involve difficult decisions. Death will occur quickly if CPR is not begun immediately. For some, it will be futile, possibly harmful, but the benefit or harm (burden) cannot be determined with absolute certainty for any one person. The problems surrounding tube feeding are primarily emotional, rather than medical, issues. Some people believe that withholding or withdrawing tube feeding is the same as starving a person to death. Let's look at some of the medical and ethical issues involved in decisions about these two treatments.

CARDIOPULMONARY RESUSCITATION

CPR was first used to restore heartbeat and breathing in emergency situations such as drowning or other accidents, choking, and sudden heart attacks in previously healthy people. As CPR technology has developed, the use of it has expanded to include many cardiac or respiratory arrest (stoppage) situations, including those that happen in hospitals and nursing homes. Now in most, if not all, hospitals and many nursing homes the policy is that CPR will be attempted if the patient's doctor has not written a No CPR, sometimes called a do-not-resuscitate (DNR) order. Remember Mrs. Wanglie? Her first respiratory arrest occurred when she was in an ambulance en route from a nursing home to a hospital. Her second, a cardiac and respiratory arrest, happened while in a chronic care hospital. She was resuscitated and transferred to the acute care hospital where she spent the rest of her life. At that time, her doctors had not written a No CPR order. Later her family consented to withholding resuscitation, even though they would not consent to withdrawing the respirator that was supporting her breathing.

CPR includes various means of trying to restart or to strengthen weak and irregular heartbeat and breathing. Neither of these two functions, breathing or heartbeat, can continue for many minutes without the other; that's why it's called cardiopulmonary resuscitation. Many of us have taken basic CPR courses and learned how to do mouth-to-mouth breathing and apply pressure to the chest. We were instructed to begin this immediately and have someone call 911 for the paramedics; they then take over with mechanical devices and a variety of means to restore cardiac and respiratory function. They may apply a bag, a type of mask, over the person's mouth to assist in breathing, or they may *intubate,* which means inserting a tube into the person's throat so that mechanically assisted breathing can be started. This means putting the person on a respirator, sometimes called a ventilator, which we'll discuss later. The paramedics also may inject drugs or apply electric shock, or both, and then transport the person to a hospital emergency room.

Cardiopulmonary function keeps the brain supplied with the oxygen it needs to function. If heartbeat or breathing stops for a few minutes, the brain can be permanently damaged, depending upon the length of time between the arrest and the resuscitation and the general health of the person. Overall, about 1 in 20 CPR attempts results in severe and irreversible brain damage,[1] although CPR procedures and technology are being modified and expanded continually to be more effective and less harmful.

For most people with advanced chronic disease or advanced cancer, CPR has been found to be ineffective. Studies show that on average, fewer than 10 percent of patients with such conditions who have been resuscitated live to leave the hospital. For people in nursing homes, the effectiveness rate is even lower and the risk of harm greater,[2] because residents of nursing homes are more likely to have chronic illnesses and nursing homes lack the advanced CPR equipment that hospitals have, so the probability of successful resuscitation is less in a nursing home. Also, nursing homes have fewer nurses and nursing assistants per patient than acute care hospitals do, so the chances of a resident having an unobserved arrest are higher. This means a longer delay in beginning CPR and a greater possibility of brain damage. Other harm includes bones broken during CPR, because nursing home residents tend to be frail. People receiving home care have many of the same characteristics and face similar risks.

Recognition of the ineffectiveness and harm of CPR for chronically ill people has produced another ethical dilemma. Should a physician get informed consent for a No CPR order if he or she believes that CPR will be ineffective for, even harmful to, the patient? On the one hand, reasonable medical practice requires physicians to use their judgment regarding treatment that will be effective for a particular disease condition; they are not required to provide futile treatment. On the other hand, the physician can never be 100 percent certain that the treatment will be futile, and withholding CPR means that the patient will certainly die within minutes. Shouldn't a patient or the patient's proxy be given information about the potential harm and benefit and then be allowed to make the decision? Some people may want to take the chance, even if the possibility of benefit is low, so that they may have a bit more time; others want to make the decision themselves, to maintain control. Some may want either a doctor or a proxy to decide. There are some doctors who believe that the decision process itself is harmful; others believe that patient/proxy self-determination is best. This is not a simple question with easy answers, which is why it's especially important to talk with your doctor about CPR.

Here are some questions to ask when you meet with your doctor to discuss your advance directive:

1. Do you write No CPR orders?
2. At what point would your write a No CPR order for me?
3. Would you discuss the chances of resuscitation (CPR) with me or my proxy before writing a No CPR order?
4. Would you write a No CPR order if I were not in a hospital or nursing home?
5. If I should happen to be intubated and placed on a respirator, would you stop the respirator if I would never be able to breathe on my own?
6. If I had a No CPR order and had to have surgery, would the order be honored during surgery and recovery?

Asking these questions will give you more information about your doctor's feelings, experiences, and practice related to resuscitation. It will give your doctor information about your concerns. Let's look at some of the issues underlying these questions.

Writing a No CPR Order

Most hospitals and nursing homes are required to have policies about resuscitation decisions; most require written No CPR orders if CPR is not to be done. Some nursing homes want either a CPR or a No CPR order written at the time of admission or shortly afterward so that the nurses will know what to do if a cardiopulmonary arrest occurs. There are still a few physicians who refuse to issue a written order. Nursing home administrators tell about the occasional doctor who either feels there is a legal risk in writing such an order or wants to wait a while before making a decision. The first reason is not valid; the second one is, unless the person has a condition in which an arrest might occur at any time. One reason for delay is that a doctor may feel that the person and family need more time to think about the decision. If, however, the person has an advance directive stating that no CPR is to be done, and the directive has been accepted and placed in the medical record, the doctor should either honor the person's wishes and write a No CPR order or offer to withdraw as the person's physician. To do otherwise, unless there is a strong indication that a No CPR order is not within the limits of reasonable medical practice, is not reasonable medical practice.

When the No CPR Order Is Written

Most living will laws require that the declarant be in a terminal condition before life-sustaining treatment can be withheld or withdrawn. Many of the chronic conditions for which CPR is not effective would not meet the restrictive definitions of terminal conditions in some state laws. For example, a person with congestive heart disease, advanced pulmonary (respiratory) disease, chronic kidney disease, or incurable cancer may not want CPR attempted in the event of a cardiac or pulmonary arrest. These conditions may not meet the imminent death requirement in that person's state living will law. Therefore, physician judgment is the primary determinant as to when a No CPR order will be written. Some physicians may follow the futility standard and write a No CPR order even though the patient's condition may not be terminal under the definition in the law. Others may not. This is an important matter to discuss with your doctor.

Discussing a No CPR Order

Whether the doctor discusses the No CPR order with the patient or the proxy depends upon both the patient and the doctor. The doctor's preference can reveal major differences between her or his beliefs and those of the patient. Such differences can erode trust, and trust is essential to the tranquillity that most of us hope will surround our final days. If you both agree that the No CPR decision will be made jointly, fine. If you both agree that the doctor should make the decision, based on medical futility, fine; if neither you nor your proxy wants to make the decision, you should not be forced to do so. If you and your doctor disagree, however, try to resolve your differences in advance. If they cannot be resolved, you may decide to transfer to another doctor, or your doctor may decide to recommend that you transfer.

NO CPR ORDERS IN HOME CARE

When my father-in-law, at age 88, was in the last stages of congestive heart disease, he was still able to live at home, even though he was weak, short of breath, and receiving oxygen through a tube. His doctor wrote a No CPR order, which Dad signed. The home health nurse put it on the refrigerator door, underneath his medication list. His granddaughter, who lived with him during the last month of his life, left the house for a short errand one day. When she returned, she found him peacefully sleeping in his rocking chair, his beloved dog at his side. He was not breathing, nor could she feel his pulse. As previously agreed, she called the family, rather than 911, because the doctor had notified the county coroner of the No CPR order. We gathered round, wept, said our good-byes, and then called the undertaker who came and took Dad's body for cremation.

Now that more people are receiving home health care, the question of honoring No CPR orders in the home is being raised more often. A few communities have developed emergency medical services policies to address home No CPR orders. We felt that Dad was fortunate to live in such a community and to have a physician who was willing to write the No CPR order. Even if we had called 911, the paramedics would not have been required to start CPR because the doctor had left a written order. Most such policies require a specific form, and the home health nurse makes sure it is available to the paramedics; it's typically fastened to the refrigerator door along with other medical information. The doctor files a copy of the form with the county coroner, because in most, if not all, states, when someone dies outside of a hospital or nursing home, the coroner must investigate to make sure that death was from natural causes.

You may wonder why the paramedics would be called when there is a No CPR order or when someone is obviously dead. There are several reasons: the person who finds the body may be distressed and call 911 in panic, may not be sure the person is dead, or may not know what to do about the body. An advance directive is not the same as a No CPR order, however, so in the absence of a written order from the doctor, even if there were a directive saying that the person did not want CPR, the paramedics would probably begin resuscitation efforts.

Most No CPR policies only apply when people are under home health or hospice care. If you do not want CPR under any circumstances, ask your doctor about the policy of the emergency medical services in your state or community and about your options if there is no policy. You should also discuss your feelings with your family and close neighbors, if you live alone. Should you tell them not to call 911 if you were to collapse, for example? Probably not, because this places a responsibility on them to make both a medical and a legal determination. But ask your doctor to ensure that life-support efforts will not be continued in the emergency room, if that is your wish.

Some people carry cards saying that they have a living will. This is not the same as a No CPR order; it merely alerts anyone who might find the person unconscious of the *existence* of an advance directive; it does not say anything about its *content*. If you carry such a card, be sure that it contains your proxy's name, address, and phone number.

Do-Not-Intubate Decisions and Orders

Sometimes a doctor will write No CPR and do-not-intubate (DNI) orders together. This has resulted in confusion regarding the intent of a (DNI) order in an emergency situation. DNI means "Do not intubate for the purpose of long-term assisted ventilation," which means that a tube should not be inserted in the throat for the purpose of putting someone on a respirator to maintain breathing indefinitely. In an emergency, paramedics may insert a tube into the throat for the purpose of resuscitation—to attempt to establish breathing—and a decision must be made later to withdraw it. Remember that we talked earlier about how it may be more difficult to withdraw treatment than to withhold it. If you do not want to be on a respirator, tell your doctor that and write in your directive, "I do not want to be kept alive on a respirator when I cannot breathe on my own." Even if you were to be intubated and placed on a respirator in an emergency situation, your doctor, in accordance with your wishes, should issue the order to withdraw the respirator. The one exception would be if you wanted to donate your organs after death; then your body might be kept on the respirator until brain death was determined and your organs removed. We'll discuss organ donation later.

NO CPR ORDERS AND SURGERY

Some hospitals have a policy that No CPR orders will not be honored during and immediately after major surgery, especially when general anesthesia is used. This is because, for some people, there may be an increased possibility of cardiopulmonary arrest during this time. Others may ask patients who have a No CPR order to sign a release from the order or to sign a special No CPR consent form to cover an arrest during surgery. If your doctor has written a No CPR order for you and you are later advised to have surgery, be sure to ask about the policy in the hospital where the surgery is to be performed. Ask before you consent to the surgery and ask both your doctor and the surgeon, if the surgeon is not your regular doctor. Ask your doctor and the surgeon about the benefits and risks of the surgery and of CPR; be sure that both doctors know your wishes and that you know whether or not they will be honored during and immediately after surgery. You may have to decide whether to consent to the surgery or to suspension of the No CPR order.

ARTIFICIALLY ADMINISTERED NUTRITION AND HYDRATION (TUBE FEEDING)

Tube feeding is usually called *artificial* or *artificially administered nutrition and hydration,* sometimes *artificial sustenance.* It does *not* mean food and water taken by mouth—eating and drinking. Tube feeding means providing nutrients and fluids through tubes that are inserted into a person's stomach through the nose (nasogastric or NG tube) or surgically inserted into the stomach (gastrostomy) or, less frequently, into the small intestine (jejunostomy). As a rule, tube feeding decisions are not about intravenous (IV) administration of fluids, nutrients, and medications. IV administration is usually short-term, because most people's veins will not tolerate long-term use; IVs are not usually used for nutritional purposes in nursing homes or home health care. In a special type of IV administration, called *total parental nutrition* (TPN), tubes are inserted into a large vein in the chest or neck for longer-term use than an IV. TPN is rarely used in terminal care, because it is more expensive and requires more intensive nursing care than NG and gastrostomy feedings. The intent of all three is the same: to provide nourishment and fluids to people who are unable to take them by mouth. We will focus on long-term tube feeding for people who are unable to eat or drink because of an incurable or irreversible disease.

Decisions to refuse tube feeding often are accompanied by strong emotions and controversy; some have ended up in court. As we learned earlier, a number of state living will laws have special provisions and prohibitions about tube feeding decisions. They reflect the value that our society places on food as a part of our religious and social values: feeding the hungry, serving food and drink to visitors, and feasting as part of family gatherings and church and community celebrations. Restrictions in the living will laws also are based on a lack of understanding of the nutritional needs of people at the end of life, the physiology of dying, and the comparative benefits and burdens of tube feedings.

If you decide that you do not want tube feeding, you may face opposition from your family. A woman who was preparing her living will asked me the following question: "Is it true that the law says I cannot refuse tube feeding? I am going to make my daughter my proxy, and when I told her that I don't want tube feeding, she said that she could never consent to starve me to death. Then she said that she'd never have to make such a decision anyhow, because it is against the law to withhold or withdraw a feeding tube. Is that true?" I told her that it was not true, that under Minnesota's living will law declarants can (the law says "must") either state their wishes about tube feeding or state that they want the proxy to make the decision. But I advised her to talk with her daughter some more and explain her wishes; perhaps she was placing too heavy a burden on her daughter, given her daughter's feelings. The woman said, "Oh, I guess I'll just name my other daughter as my proxy!" It's not an easy task to talk with loved ones about withholding treatment; it's even more difficult when the treatment is tube feeding.

It is helpful to be prepared with medical and ethical facts about tube feeding, both in making your decision and in explaining it to others. Let's look at some of the misunderstandings and some of the medical, ethical, and legal issues related to tube feeding.

The Starvation Myth

You may be told, if you decide to refuse tube feeding, "It's wrong to starve people to death!" Few would disagree. But advance directives are not about deliberately starving a healthy person. They are about a medical treatment decision when the disease process has progressed to the point where a person is unable to take food and water by mouth, perhaps because he or she is unconscious or otherwise unable to swallow. In this stage, the body's nutritional needs diminish and the chemical balance changes; accompanying dehydration may result in progressive loss of consciousness.

A related question that often comes up when discussing tube feeding is, "Is it painful to die without it? Won't I suffer from hunger or thirst?" Perhaps the questioners have never been with a dying person, have never seen how the body begins to shut down as death approaches. There may be pain and discomfort from other sources. These should be controlled with pain relief measures and comfort care. In persistent vegetative state (PVS), the condition in which tube feeding most frequently becomes an issue, a person is not able to feel pain because the pain areas of the brain no longer function. PVS has been the diagnosis in most of the court cases in which withdrawing tube feeding has been the issue. Remember Mrs. Browning's case? Although she died while on the feeding tube, others such as Paul Brophy[3] in Massachusetts and Nancy Cruzan in Missouri[4] have had the feeding tube withdrawn and have died peacefully with their families at their bedsides. This is the most important consideration: that if tube feeding—or any other life-sustaining treatment—is withheld or withdrawn, you will not be abandoned. Reasonable medical practice, and law, require that appropriate care be given. Appropriate care of dying people is the humane principal on which hospice care is founded.

Benefits and Burdens of Tube Feeding

Tube feeding is a medical treatment, even though some state laws say that it is not and define it as "comfort care." Tube feeding requires a physician's order; inserting the tube is a medical procedure, including surgery for a gastrostomy tube, that requires skilled personnel; skilled nursing care is required to prevent complications. The American Medical Association's Council on Ethical and Judicial Affairs has placed tube feeding in perspective for physicians:

> Life-prolonging treatment includes medications and artificially or technologically supplied respiration, nutrition, or hydration. In treating a terminally ill or irreversibly comatose patient, the physician should determine whether the benefits of the treatment outweigh its burdens. At all times the dignity of the patient should be maintained.[5]

Sometimes tube feeding is begun because a person is not eating, is losing weight, growing weaker. If the doctor believes that this is a temporary condition, the intent is to try tube feeding for a relatively short period because it is medically necessary for recovery or to reverse the condition. Under these circumstances, if the patient or proxy consents, inserting a feeding tube would be considered reasonable medical practice. It is intended to benefit the patient. If a feeding tube is inserted without consent when there is no possibility of recovery, as in properly diagnosed PVS, it is not reasonable medical practice, even though if may conform to a particular state's law.

Federal and state nursing home regulations have reinforced tube feeding by setting daily caloric and nutritional standards and by using weight loss as an indicator of poor treatment. As a result, people who eat poorly or slowly or who require assistance to eat may have feeding tubes inserted rather than helping them eat and drink or trying to determine the reason for their inability or unwillingness to eat or drink. Fortunately, recent federal nursing home regulations require more medical justification for tube feeding, so there may be a change in medical practice over time.[6]

Feeding tubes can result in medical harm, including fluid and electrolyte (chemical) disturbances, aspiration pneumonia, diarrhea or constipation, and irritation of the nose and throat with the NG tube or infection at the site where the gastrostomy tube is inserted. Some people have to be restrained—have their hands tied down—to prevent them from pulling out their feeding tubes. Most of these complications can be prevented by careful monitoring of the patient and good nursing care.

Ethical and legal, rather than medical, issues are the primary concerns surrounding tube feeding. As a result, families and health care providers may turn to the courts when there is disagreement about withdrawing a feeding tube. It was a factor in the passage of the federal Patient Self-Determination Act of 1990 (PSDA) with its renewed emphasis on the importance of advance directives to protect and promote self-determination.

Giles Scofield, a lawyer and biomedical ethicist, advocates use of the "least restrictive alternative" when feeding decisions are being made. He writes:

> Of all the reasons that justify withholding or withdrawing a feeding tube, the most fundamental is that the patient does not need it (tube-feeding) in order to live or to receive adequate nourishment safely .... The responsible use of feeding tubes concerns more than knowing when patients may be permitted to die without them. It involves enabling and permitting patients to live without them.[7]

The following example illustrates the importance of Scofield's advice. I received a phone call from a hospital social worker regarding a woman who had been admitted to the hospital from a nursing home because she was neither talking nor eating. She had been diagnosed as severely depressed and was given electric shock treatments, which helped her.[8] She was transferred to the hospital's rehabilitation department, where she was talking, eating, and socializing, and would soon be discharged back to the nursing home. As part of her rehabilitation workup, she was found to have problems with her vision. She had no peripheral vision and could see only what was directly in front of her. If her food tray was not properly placed and if there was not adequate lighting, she couldn't see to eat. The social worker was concerned that when the woman returned to the nursing home, she would not eat because she could not see her food and a feeding tube might be inserted. This woman had not prepared a living will, and she had no family to serve as her proxy or advocate or to visit her and help her to eat, so the possibility of tube feeding to meet medical regulations or for convenience was a valid concern. The hospital social worker phoned to request that a Medical Decisions Advocate (MDA) be assigned to assist this woman. The MDA program was a pilot program to train volunteers to serve as advocates for people without family or other proxy when urgent medical decisions had to be made.[9] I was not able to assign an MDA in this situation because there was no urgent medical decision to be made, but it illustrates the growing problem of the "unbefriended elderly"—people who don't have family or others who can serve as their health care proxies. In this case, neither of the alternatives that we arrived at was reassuring. The first was that the hospital social worker would talk with the woman's doctor and the nursing home social worker to make sure that they were aware of the woman's poor vision and that the staff would place her tray properly in front of her and help her to eat, if necessary. We were not confident that this would be sufficient, especially over a long period. The other alternative was to seek a court-appointed guardian, but a guardian would probably refuse tube feeding because of the misunderstanding of the medical and legal issues surrounding it. In addition, under guardianship the woman would lose some of her right to self-determination, although in her current situation she was not able or had not been permitted to exercise it. The social worker was planning to discuss the possibility of an advance directive with the woman so that her wishes would be known.

The Courts and Tube Feeding

The least restrictive alternative doctrine, which Scofield advocates for nutrition and hydration decisions, is based on a person's constitutional right to liberty. In the Nancy Cruzan decision, the United States Supreme Court, even though it upheld the Missouri Supreme Court decision that the feeding tube that was keeping Nancy alive could not be withdrawn under Missouri's law, stated that people have a liberty right to refuse medical treatment. The Court held that Missouri had the authority to require "clear and convincing" evidence of a person's wishes, however, and that this standard had not been met.[10] Nancy Cruzan did not have a written directive.

Even though the U.S. Supreme Court did not rule that Nancy's feeding tube should be removed, following the decision, her parents went back to the county court in Missouri. This court, as it had done three years earlier, authorized stopping the feedings. The tube was removed, and Nancy died peacefully 12 days later, nearly 7 years after the automobile accident that left her permanently unconscious.

Even in light of the Supreme Court decision, many doctors remain reluctant to withhold or withdraw tube feeding. In a survey done after the Cruzan decision, Missouri physicians were asked if they would recommend tube feeding in the hypothetical case of an 89-year-old man who had had a severe stroke one week earlier and was not able to swallow or to communicate. Half of the 439 doctors surveyed were told that he had prepared a standard living will that did not specifically refuse tube feeding; the other half were told that he had a living will that specifically refused tube feeding. In the first situation, more than half (58%) of the doctors said they would recommend tube feeding. When they thought that the man's living will specifically refused tube feeding, 47% still said they would recommend it. Family wishes were an important factor in the physicians' decisions, as was the patient's age; they were more likely to recommend feedings for younger people. If there was no improvement in the patient's medical condition after a year, half opposed tube feeding, but it was not clear if they would withdraw the tube.[11] This study shows the importance of both a specific directive regarding your wishes about tube feeding and discussing your wishes with family and doctor.

What can you do in the face of the complex, confusing, and conflicting mixture of emotional, medical, ethical, and legal issues that surrounds tube feeding? First, think about tube feeding as a medical treatment and subject it to the same criteria to which you would subject any other treatment. Ask yourself, "What will the results of my decision be?" With tube feeding you can be kept alive indefinitely; without it you will die—usually within a week or two, depending upon your overall condition. Next, talk with your family, especially the person you are thinking about asking to be your proxy, your doctor, and perhaps your minister, priest, or rabbi. Then write down your wishes and instructions, based on your contemplation and your conversations. You might write, "I want tube feeding (artificial nutrition and hydration) if I have a temporary condition in which I cannot eat or drink *and* every effort has been made to help me take food and water by mouth *and* the prospects of my recovery from this condition are good. If I do not recover from this condition, I want the feeding tube withdrawn (or continued)."

Or you might write, "I never want tube feeding begun." Or "I do not want tube feeding if I am in a persistent vegetative state (or permanently unconscious)."

You can state, "I want my proxy (or my doctor) to make decisions about tube feeding consistent with my other instructions and wishes." I do not recommend this, however, because it places them in a difficult situation. We've discussed the strong emotions surrounding tube feeding, and I do not believe it is fair to place the burden for such a decision, whether it is to provide or withhold tube feeding, on another person. Also, if you do not want tube feeding, the possibility of your decision not being honored is greater if you do not specifically state it.

OTHER MEDICAL TREATMENTS

Respirators (Breathing Machines)

Respirators, sometimes called *ventilators*, are mechanical devices that either assist or take over the exchange of air for people who, because of disease, injury, or death (brain death) cannot breathe for themselves. The iron lungs of 50 years ago were respirators. The modern versions are smaller and some are portable so that a person can carry on daily living activities while on the respirator. A person is connected to the respirator by a tube that enters the body either through the nose and mouth or through a surgical incision in the throat (tracheostomy). A respirator can be used for short periods to help a person breathe until he or she is able to resume breathing independently. Respirators also can sustain life, or prolong dying, for long periods.

Karen Ann Quinlan was on a respirator in a persistent vegetative state for more than a year following a respiratory arrest at age 20. In March 1976, the New Jersey Supreme Court supported her parents' request to withdraw the respirator, reversing the decision of a lower court.[12] Karen Ann did not die, however, but continued to live for nine more years on a feeding tube.

Morphine Administration when Withdrawing a Respirator

Morphine is often given before a respirator is removed because the dying person can experience severe difficulty breathing when the respirator is removed. Even if the patient is unconscious and does not feel pain, this gasping (agonal) breathing is difficult for families and others who are at the deathbed. Two Minnesota cases illustrate some ethical, legal, and practical issues related to the administration of morphine to dying people and why fear of legal action can result in diminished pain control. These two cases involved dying people who were on respirators in two different hospitals; both were receiving morphine for pain. One case involved a young man with a rare and incurable autoimmune disease. Bone marrow transplant therapy had been tried and was ineffective. He asked to have the respirator removed and be allowed to die, and his family agreed. He was given a large dose of morphine, the respirator was removed, and he died quickly and peacefully.

The second case involved a woman who was dying of cancer. She was unconscious and was given an extremely large dose of morphine. Her respirator was removed with family consent. One of the nurses, who was concerned by the large dose of morphine used, discussed it with the hospital's medical director. Hospital policy required notification of the county medical examiner (coroner) in such a situation. The medical examiner and the county attorney launched an investigation and found that there was no state law or formal policy to guide medical practice related to the use of morphine in such situations. They recommended that practice guidelines be developed.[13] No criminal charges were filed against the doctors or hospitals involved, but the resulting publicity reportedly made some physicians unwilling to order adequate morphine to control pain in dying patients. Other doctors said they would continue to order as much pain medication as was needed to keep their patients comfortable, that their ethical and legal duty was to the welfare of their patients.

Respirators, Brain Death, and Organ Transplantation

Before mechanical respirators were developed, a person was considered dead when the heart had stopped beating and breathing had ceased. When the body is on a respirator, however, both cardiac and respiratory function continue mechanically, and death is determined by medical tests that show no remaining function of the entire brain. These tests are repeated over a period ranging from 6 to 24 hours, depending on the type of test used. Brain death is not the same as persistent vegetative state, in which the lower part of the brain, the brain stem, continues to function. A person who is brain dead is dead. Several people have said to me, "I would like to donate my organs after I die, but I am afraid they'll take them before I die." Be assured that strict requirements govern organ donation and that the laws that govern organ donation are separate from living will laws. They require consent of the next of kin or legal guardian. The order of consent is usually guardian, spouse, adult children for older people, parents of children, siblings, other relatives. Most durable power of attorney for health care laws neither permit the agent to nor prohibit the agent from consenting to organ donation, although Tennessee's law specifically gives the agent power to authorize an autopsy; donate organs or the entire body or parts of it for transplantation, therapeutic, educational, or scientific purposes; and dispose of the remains. (We'll discuss that last matter in Chapter 6.)

Some states, in an effort to increase the supply of donated organs, require hospitals to request organ donation if a person who might be a qualified donor is admitted in a condition in which death is expected to occur within a short time. A qualified organ donor is usually a person under age 60 whose organs are in good enough condition to benefit another. Often such a person has been injured in an accident, placed on a respirator, and pronounced brain dead. The organs most frequently donated are kidney, heart, heart and lungs, liver, and sometimes pancreas, although research and technology continue to expand the list. These organs must be removed within a few hours after death, and the body must be kept on a respirator so that blood and oxygen are supplied to them. The cost is borne by the organ recipient or the organ transplant center, not by the donor.

Other body parts and tissues, such as cornea, skin, and connective tissue can also be used for the benefit or others; the maximum age for donors is higher than that for organs. Medical schools accept donations of the entire body after death; your doctor, your state medical association, or a medical school should be able to give you more information about this.

How does organ donation apply to an advance directive? It is another end-of-life decision and it is best made by you before death, even though consent must be given after death by another person. Stating your wishes concerning organ and tissue donation in your advance directive will assist your family or other proxy. If they know your wishes, they will be better prepared to consent or refuse, should they be asked to authorize organ or tissue donation or an autopsy.

Autopsy is another after-death procedure. It is legally required in some situations, such as when there is suspicion of "unnatural death," in which case consent is not necessary. In other situations, your doctor may believe that autopsy would benefit others by enabling doctors to learn more about a disease or cause of death.

It can be immensely helpful to your loved ones if they know your wishes about organ donation and autopsy. Their grief or, in the case of a sudden accident, state of shock at the time of death may be such that they will not be able to make a decision, and the opportunity to benefit others will be lost. So think about organ donation and autopsy as you prepare your directive, discuss it with your family and proxy, and write your wishes in your directive. If you do not want to be on a respirator for a long period, but want to donate your organs, you should say, "I do not want long-term assisted respiration, but I authorize use of the respirator for the purpose of organ donation." You could also complete a donor card from the American Red Cross and the Lion's Club Eye Bank. You can withdraw your consent to organ donation just as you can rescind your advance directive.

Kidney Dialysis

When a person's kidneys fail, either because of primary kidney (renal) disease or as a complication of another disease, dialysis may be started. The elimination (blood cleansing) function of the kidneys is done through tubes inserted either into blood vessels or into the abdomen. Dialysis treatments, which last several hours, are done as often as necessary—perhaps three times a week in the beginning, sometimes less often as a person's body adjusts. For some patients, dialysis is followed by a kidney transplant; for others, a transplant may not be medically feasible or financially possible, although Medicare will pay for dialysis and transplants for eligible persons.

When dialysis is no longer beneficial, either because there is little chance of recovery of kidney function or because the person finds it too burdensome, or both, a decision to withdraw from dialysis must be faced. And, as we've learned, many families, doctors, and nurses, find a decision to stop treatment much more difficult than a decision not to start treatment.

A nursing home case, described to me by the social worker who was involved, illustrates one type of dilemma faced in a decision to withdraw dialysis. A relatively young woman of 55 was a resident in a nursing home because she was unable to care for herself and needed nursing care. She had chronic heart and kidney disease and had been receiving dialysis on a weekly basis for more than a year. She knew that a kidney transplant was not medically feasible for her. Finally, she decided that the quality of her life was not worth the discomfort, and she asked her doctor to stop the dialysis. She had seven adult children; they were notified of her decision, and several months of intense disagreement followed. Each child insisted that he or she should be the decision maker. Some agreed with their mother's decision; others did not. Each claimed authority to make the decision. They kept contacting the nursing home staff, their mother, and her doctor until, when it became apparent that there would be no resolution of the conflict among the children, the doctor honored the woman's decision. He knew that she was competent to make the decision for herself, and he respected her right to make it, even though it would lead to her death.

In this situation, had the mother prepared an advance directive and discussed her wishes with her children, it might not have made a difference; it was a fractious family. Moreover, as long as the woman was competent to make her own decision, the directive would not have been operative. Had she slipped into a coma, however, or had her doctor and the nursing home staff not been so courageous in the face of family disagreement, there might have been a longer period of conflict, perhaps even involving court action.

Another case illustrates the discomfort that both family members and health care providers may feel about decisions to stop treatment. It, too, involved kidney dialysis, although similar situations can arise with any treatment for a chronic disease, especially if it is not considered terminal. I received a call from a county adult protection worker asking to have a Medical Decisions Advocate (MDA) assigned to assist a man, Mr. B, who had been receiving kidney dialysis once a week for several years. Several weeks ago, Mr. B stopped coming to the hospital for his dialysis treatment. His kidney disease was accompanied by other chronic health problems, so he was receiving home health care as well. He was in his mid-50s, had never married, and had been living with a brother, who had died a year earlier. He had a niece and nephew who visited him occasionally but apparently were not closely involved in his life. Mr. B told his public health nurse that he did not want to live any longer and that he had been told that if he stopped dialysis he would die. In addition, he was beginning to question the need for dialysis, because it had been three weeks since his last treatment and he was still alive.

The nurse asked the county adult protection agency to request a legally appointed guardian to make health care decisions for Mr. B. The nurse felt that his decision, which would probably result in his death, was wrong. She felt he was too depressed to make a rational choice. Because it was not a clear case of either abuse or neglect (self-neglect of health is one of the reasons guardianship might be considered) and there were family members available to serve as private guardians, the county adult protection agency did not deem it appropriate to petition for guardianship. The nurse met with Mr. B's niece and nephew, but neither wanted to become involved in medical decision making, either as an informal proxy or as a private court-appointed guardian. That was when the county social worker phoned me to request that an MDA be assigned to Mr. B. This seemed to be an urgent situation, so I assigned a specially trained volunteer, a public health nurse, to the case. She met with Mr. B several times and also met with his public health nurse and staff members from the kidney dialysis center. All decided that Mr. B was able to exercise informed consent or, in this case, refusal. The public health nurse was willing to accept his decision, even though she personally did not agree with it. (I do not know the outcome of the case because, for privacy reasons, the MDA assignment was limited to the time required to assist and advocate through the decision making process.)

How does this case apply to advance directives? Not only does it show the many different feelings involved when a person decides to stop or to refuse life-sustaining treatment, but it illustrates the problem of people without family or close friends to serve as health decision proxies. An advance directive is especially important in such situations. A written declaration will help whoever is involved when decisions must be made to exercise substitute judgment—to decide as the person would have decided. A directive is especially helpful if a guardian is appointed to make medical decisions, particularly when the decisions are about withholding or withdrawing life-sustaining treatment.

Both of these cases are reminders of the tragic element of medical decisions involving life-sustaining treatment and of terminal illness. Here were two relatively young people for whom medical treatment, in this case kidney dialysis, could not cure their disease; it could only prolong life. Both made the decision that such a life was not worth the burden it imposed upon them. Others felt differently and were troubled by the decision; caregivers and family members expressed their feelings in different ways. The emotions surrounding terminal illness are evidence of the concern and dedication that caregivers—doctors, nurses, nursing assistants, social workers, chaplains, and others—have for those in their care. Death affects all.

Other Treatments and Procedures

We have examined some of the treatments that are usually thought of as life-sustaining. Most medical treatments will be life-sustaining at some point in some person's life; they can also become unduly burdensome. They may only postpone death or prolong suffering. Examples include antibiotics to fight infection, surgery such as a limb amputation due to gangrene in legs and feet where blood flow has failed, and chemotherapy in the final stages of cancer. Blood transfusions can also be futile, even burdensome, as can some diagnostic procedures. The time comes when death must be accepted, and the plan of care focused on comfort and support, rather than treatment. In Chapter 6, we'll discuss some statements that you can make in your directive about the conditions under which you would want or not want these various treatments.

NECESSARY TREATMENT, THERAPY, AND CARE

Rehabilitation Assessment and Therapies

Too often, attention is focused on life-sustaining treatment and the right to refuse it. But even though you prepare an advance directive and state that you do not want life-*sustaining* treatment, you still have a right to life-*enhancing* treatment. There are some therapies that can make it possible to continue the activities of daily life and to live at home or in the least restrictive type of residential care. Access to these therapies and services may require assertiveness on your part or assertive advocacy by your proxy.

Assessment for rehabilitation potential should be done and the needed services provided, as long as they will benefit you. Among such services are speech, physical, occupational, and respiratory therapy; mental health services; and vision, hearing, and dental assessment and services. These therapies and services should be provided but sometimes are not. Physicians, caregivers, and families may not realize the potential of the person to benefit from them, or health insurance may not adequately reimburse for such services, although Medicare will pay for some rehabilitation in some settings, including therapy provided through a Medicare-certified home care agency. If you state in your directive that you want the therapy, care, and support services necessary to keep you as active and independent as possible, you will be reminding your doctor to consider them and your proxy to advocate them, should you be unable to do so.

Hospice Care

Hospice is both a philosophy of care and a service provider. The philosophy is to provide care appropriate to the needs of a dying person and those close to them. Dame Cicely Saunders, who founded the first modern hospice program, St. Christopher's Hospital in London, summarizes the hospice philosophy well:

> You matter because you are you. You matter to the last moment of your life, and we will do all we can not only to help you die peacefully, but also to live until you die.[14]

Hospice care provides assurance of appropriate care during the final period of life. Not all doctors are familiar with the benefits of hospice, however, so, again, you may have to be assertive or have an assertive proxy. When my mother-in-law was in the final stages of cancer, I suggested to her doctor that we consider hospice care. He replied, "That is only for the last two weeks of life" and refused to consider it. Instead, he ordered her into the hospital. My father-in-law said, "The doctor knows best" and consented to hospitalization. After three days, she was transferred to a nursing home where she died five and a half months later. She was not unhappy in the nursing home and received adequate care, but her husband never had a chance to prepare for her death, to be involved in her care and in her dying. He was not with her when she died. Had she been in hospice care it is more likely that he, or some of the family, would have been at her bedside in the last moments of her life.

The typical hospice period is six months, but it can be longer. At this writing (1992) Medicare will pay for hospice care, except for some charges for inpatient respite care and outpatient drugs. Hospice services are not only for patients with cancer. Although most hospice patients are dying of cancer, others with terminal conditions such as AIDS, are now being served. Hospice services can be provided in a facility, but more often the person is able to remain at home where hospice nurses and volunteers and family are all involved in the care. Intermittent hospital care may be available if the person needs it or the family needs respite. The hospice philosophy can and should be applied in any setting, especially since eight out of ten deaths occur in either a hospital or a nursing home. Unfortunately, this is not always achieved.

It's important to talk with your doctor and your family about hospice care and to learn about the hospice programs in your community. Most hospice programs are listed in the phone directory, or you can contact your hospital or public health nursing agency for information. Be sure to ask if the program is Medicare-certified.

Management of Pain

Adequate pain management is a part of the hospice philosophy, but it should be practiced wherever and whenever pain is experienced. Fear of pain adds to the suffering of dying people and their families; it can make actual pain more intense. Although pain management is more than giving medication to control pain, you can make some specific statements about medication in your directive to encourage your doctor and nurses to give you adequate medication, including morphine, as necessary to control pain.

Giving large doses of morphine to control pain, even though it may hasten death, illustrates the ethical principle of *double effect,* which is also described in the Vatican Declaration on Euthanasia: If the intent of an act is moral and if there is no other way to achieve the desired effect, relief of pain, but an unintended effect is death, the act is moral nevertheless. To offset concern of legal risk on the part of my caregivers, I wrote in my living will, "I want adequate pain medication given to me if I suffer from pain even though this will hasten my death."

Occasionally, some one will express a concern that giving large quantities of narcotics to control pain in a dying person will result in the person becoming addicted. This may seem a ridiculous fear, but be prepared for it. Point out that when a person is dying, if the alternative is severe pain and suffering, addiction can be regarded as a lesser evil.

NURSING HOME CARE

Many people, when preparing an advance directive, have asked, "Can I say that I never want to be in a nursing home?" My response is, "You can write whatever you wish. You might want to consider two things, however. First, there are many fine nursing homes. The quality of life is not necessarily poor, and some people find companionship in nursing homes. My mother-in-law did. She liked being around lots of people and was able to join in some group activities.

Another consideration is that if your family were not able to care for you at home, how would they feel if you had written, "I never want to be in a nursing home?"

You should consider whether or not you would want to be transferred to a hospital for treatment if you are in a nursing home when you are terminally ill. One reason for transferring someone to the hospital is cardio-pulmonary arrest. If your doctor has written a No CPR order, in accordance with your wishes, the paramedics would not be called, and you would not be sent to the emergency room. Other reasons for transfer include pneumonia or other infection, medical tests, and surgery. Even though you state your wishes about the various treatments, you could also state, "I do not (or do) want to be transferred to a hospital for treatment." This is sometimes called a do-not-hospitalize (DHI) order.

We've now discussed the first steps to take in preparing an advance directive—the thinking and talking process and some of the medical treatments to think about in preparing a "clear and convincing" statement of your wishes. In Chapter 5 we'll look at some of the issues related to selecting and being a proxy decision maker.

CHAPTER 5

PROXY DECISION MAKERS

Making decisions for someone else is a difficult task. Making life and death decisions for someone else is an awesome task. These decisions must be made, nevertheless, and when a person cannot make them, someone else, a surrogate (proxy), must decide. Advance directives not only name the proxy selected by the person but provide guidance to the proxy.

When selecting a proxy, ask yourself the following questions:

1. Who knows me well enough to understand my feelings? (Not "who do *I* know well enough," because you may find, when talking about your wishes, that you did not really know the person's feelings that well.)

2. Who is likely to be available to make medical treatment decisions when I am no longer able to make them?

3. Who is strong enough, assertive enough, to serve as my advocate?

After you have gone through this thought process, you may have several candidates, one candidate, or none. If you have more than one, talk with each of them about your wishes. At this point, your wishes and instructions about care and treatment should be relatively clear; perhaps you've already written them out. Go through them with each proxy candidate, ask how each feels about them and whether he or she would be willing to carry them out, should you not be able to speak for yourself. Remind them all, too, that their authority would start only when you were no longer able to make health care decisions for yourself. If both or all are willing, select one (only you can make this decision) and designate the other(s) as alternate(s). Some people name more than one person as proxy, although this could mean a delay in making a decision, if both should not be available at the time or if they should not agree. I designated my husband and one of my daughters as joint proxies; my husband named me and his son. We feel this is best because ours is a second marriage for both of us and both of our families will be represented in the decision making. We are willing to risk that both will not be available if a decision must be made quickly; we are both certain that our proxies will agree and will carry out our wishes. If you choose more than one proxy, be certain that both will agree with your wishes. (A few states do not permit co-proxies, so be sure you know your state's law.) Disagreement among proxies or families is one of the primary reasons that life-sustaining treatment is provided even when it does not benefit the patient and even though there is evidence that the patient would refuse such treatment if able to do so. Fear of being sued is a powerful incentive for treatment, and proxy and family disagreements add to this fear.

What if you identify only one candidate and that person is unwilling to be your proxy or to carry out your wishes? Remember the woman whose daughter said she could not refuse tube feeding? Or what if you have no family member or close friend available? Should you ask your doctor to be your proxy? The answer depends, first, on whether your state's laws permit this; some do not. It also depends upon whether your doctor is willing to do so, whether your doctor will be available when decisions must be made, and whether you are comfortable placing all decision making authority with your doctor. You might ask your minister, priest, or rabbi or your lawyer, but if you choose a lawyer, be prepared to pay attorney fees. If you have no one to serve as proxy, you could contact the state long-term care ombudsman for advice. (See Resource section of the Appendix.) The ombudsman's office might refer you to a community guardianship program or know whether there is a volunteer medical advocacy program in your community. You could also contact a community hospice program for advice. In a situation in which a person has no family or other proxy, a written directive is even more important as a guide to those relative strangers who may have to make end-of-life medical decisions, whether as physicians or legally appointed guardians.

When you have found a proxy and completed your directive, you should periodically review your instructions with your proxy to assure that your wishes remain the same and that your proxy is still willing to carry them out. Be sure to notify your doctor and all who have copies of your directives of any changes in your proxy's address and phone number. If you decide to revoke your proxy designation for any reason, also notify your doctor and everyone who has a copy. (For more about that, see Chapter 6.)

SERVING AS A PROXY

You may be designated as a proxy for someone else or be asked to make a decision for a family member in the absence of an advance directive. I can offer some advice for those who have not been placed in this difficult position. The guiding principle, based on respect for a person and the right to self-determination, is to exercise substituted judgment, to decide as the person (the principal) would have decided. If there is no written directive, try to recall any statements the principal may have made about medical treatment, about quality of life, about death and dying, perhaps when a relative, friend, or neighbor was terminally ill or had died. If possible, talk with others who knew the principal well, try to construct the decision that he or she would make. If no such statements are remembered, think about the principal. What was important in her or his life? Was this a "take charge," active person? A quiet person, who was dependent on others? What were the principal's religious beliefs? Talk with the principal's minister, priest, rabbi, or chaplain in the hospital or nursing home. What were the principal's interests? How likely is it that he or she will be able to take part in such activities again?

You will not always encounter life and death situations when serving as a proxy. You may not even be required to make decisions, but you may have to empower the person you represent—to be a forceful advocate. This role is especially important when the person is elderly. I accompanied my mother and my mother-in-law on their medical visits. A typical situation arose when my mother went to an orthopedic specialist. He talked to me instead of her, even though she was fully capable of answering his questions and understanding the proposed surgery. I finally said, "Ask her; it's her knee."

Such experiences serve as reminders that even though the laws may state that competent people have the right to make decisions as long as they are able to do so, practice may not follow law. As a proxy, you must be constantly aware of the power you have and be careful not to use it prematurely or improperly. There may come a time, nevertheless, when you must make difficult decisions because the principal is unable to make them. Two of the most difficult ones are decisions related to life-sustaining medical treatment and admission of the principal to a nursing home.

Decisions on Medical Treatment

Again, communication is the most important factor. Talk with the doctor so that you understand the prognosis (probable outcome of the disease and treatment). You can ask to see the principal's medical records. Some state living will and durable power of attorney for health care laws specifically state that a proxy has authority to review medical records. Others state that the proxy has the same rights related to health care decisions as does the principal, thus implying access to medical records. For many of us, the information in the medical record may be so technical, or the handwriting so illegible, that interpretation will be needed. Even if you do review the medical records, it is essential that you discuss your questions and concerns with the doctor. Full and open communication between proxy and physician is the most important factor in making medical decisions for another. Although the proxy is an advocate for the principal, the physician is also an advocate. An adversarial situation between physician and proxy should be avoided; it seldom benefits the principal or any of those involved in decision making.

Developing mutual trust and understanding can be a difficult and time-consuming task, especially if the patient is being treated by several physicians for a variety of conditions. I was a member of an ethics committee in a large hospital, and one case that we reviewed illustrates this problem. The wife of a man who had died of complications of heart disease contacted the hospital's patient representative. The wife was a nurse and, even though her husband had died, she wanted his case reviewed so that other families would be spared some of the frustration and anger that she felt. The problem she experienced during her husband's final illness was that she could not determine who was in charge. He was being treated by a number of specialist physicians; some of the treatment advice seemed contradictory; treatments were ordered and done without her specific consent. She did not know the overall plan for care nor which doctor to consult for advice.

This is not an unusual situation, especially in a large hospital that may have many specialties. There should be a primary physician—usually the one who knows the patient best and the one who admits the patient to the hospital. In actual practice, however, many physicians may be involved over a short period, and patient care conferences with a family member present may not happen. Medicare payment is based on average time for a hospital stay for a specific condition, so there is pressure on doctors and hospitals to order treatment as quickly as possible, and the care planning and informed consent process may be short-changed.

Although the ethics committee was able to identify the problem, the need for a stronger role for a primary care physician, we were not able to solve it. Had the wife in this situation not known about the patient representative, her problem might never have gotten a hearing. This serves as a reminder to patients, formally appointed proxies, and family members to look for patients' rights information. Ask about the hospital's policy on patients' rights, and find out how to get in touch with the patient representative and the biomedical ethics committee.

If a Directive Is Not Honored

What if the doctor, hospital, or nursing home refuses to honor a person's wishes as stated in the directive? This situation is most likely to occur when the decision is to withhold or withdraw life-sustaining treatment, especially tube feeding. Neither the Patient Self-Determination Act nor past court decisions are an absolute guarantee that unwanted treatment will not be given.

The first step in resolving conflict is to meet with the attending physician and try to achieve resolution. Perhaps the doctor has a good medical reason for not honoring the directive at this point. Listen to these reasons; if you are still concerned or if the differences cannot be satisfactorily resolved, ask to speak with the hospital's patient representative and administrator, the nursing home administrator, social worker, or chaplain. You can also request a review by the biomedical ethics committee, if there is one. You should ask about the institution's policies regarding transfer to another physician or another hospital or nursing home. Many state living will laws require physicians and other health care providers to make "reasonable" efforts to transfer care to a provider who will honor the directive.

If none of these steps results in resolution of the conflict, you will have to decide whether to accept the treatment or take legal action. You have a moral obligation and, under living will laws, a legal duty to carry out the declarant's wishes within the limits of reasonable medical practice. The law does not state that you must take legal action; only you can make that decision. If you go to court, the person's dying may become a public spectacle; it may also be an expensive process. On the other hand, if you do not, dying may be prolonged, perhaps painful, and certainly contrary to the person's wishes. Before making a final decision, tell the doctor and the hospital or nursing home administrator that you are considering legal action. You might also contact Choice in Dying. (See Resource section of the Appendix.) This organization has provided advice and assistance to the families in several of the court cases we've referred to. You may find that the situation can be resolved without going to court.

The Case of Jean Elbaum

A family in New York did decide to go to court. The resulting decision of the New York State Supreme Court was the first in which payment for unwanted treatment was an issue, although not the primary one. Jean Elbaum, age 60, had a brain hemorrhage in June 1986 and was in a deep coma. Nasogastric tube feedings were begun. She was subsequently diagnosed as being in a persistent vegetative state and transferred to a nursing home. Before transfer, her husband was told that no nursing home would accept her unless a gastrostomy tube were inserted. (A few nursing homes may still have such policies, so be sure to ask about tube feeding requirements before admission.) Her family was reluctant to consent to the gastrostomy, because Mrs. Elbaum had said that she did not want to be kept alive by machines or as a "vegetable." She had not prepared an advance directive. (New York does not have a living will law. It now has a health proxy law but did not when Mrs. Elbaum was alive.) Mr. Elbaum was told that if he did not consent to the gastrostomy, the hospital would obtain court approval, so he gave consent. His wife was transferred to a nursing home in September, three months after her stroke. Mr. Elbaum consented to a DNR order and asked that his wife not be treated with antibiotics should she develop an infection. The nursing home did not honor his request. One year later, Mr. Elbaum wrote to the medical director and to the administrator of the nursing home and asked that the gastrostomy tube be removed. His request was denied, and Mr. Elbaum stopped paying the nursing home for her care. In June 1988, two years after his wife's stroke, Mr. Elbaum began legal action to stop all life-sustaining treatment. The trial court denied his request on the basis that there was not sufficient evidence to show that Mrs. Elbaum did not want tube feeding. It also ruled that Mr. Elbaum must pay the nursing home for her care.

The decision was appealed to the New York Supreme Court, which reversed the trial court's decision, finding that various statements Mrs. Elbaum had made to family and friends were "clear and convincing" evidence of her wishes. Mrs. Elbaum was transferred to a hospice, the tube feeding was stopped, and she died peacefully. The trial court later reversed its ruling about payment for care, so Mr. Elbaum was not required to pay the remaining bills.[1]

Decisions on Nursing Home Care

Before this decision is made, explore alternatives such as home health care, a share-the-home program, or a live-in personal care attendant. These alternatives may serve for a time, but at some point the principal may need both medical and nursing care and will be hospitalized. Under current law, Medicare will pay for a certain amount of nursing home care if the person has been hospitalized for at least three days. (See Chapter 7.) Medicare pays only a fixed amount for each type of hospitalization, called Diagnosis Related Groups or DRGs, regardless of the length of stay, so physicians are under pressure to discharge patients from the hospital as soon as possible. Therefore, you may have to make a decision relatively quickly. Before consenting to transfer the principal to a nursing home, get advice about the homes available. You can ask the hospital social worker or phone the state health or human services department, the state agency on aging, or the state long-term care ombudsman program. (See Resource section of the Appendix.) Visit several nursing homes. Ask about their policies related to honoring advance directives. If there is no directive, how will decisions about life-sustaining treatment be made? What are the home's policies on resuscitation, tube feeding, on transfer to a hospital for medical treatment?

Once you decide on a nursing home, remain as actively involved in care and decisions about care as you can. *Your most important role is to assure that the principal is regarded as the decision maker to the greatest extent possible.* It is easy to assume the role of decision maker prematurely.

The Care Plan

The National Nursing Home Reform Act requires that a plan of care, based on an assessment of the resident's needs and abilities, be developed for each resident in a nursing home. Assessments must be done within 14 days of admission to the home and at least once a year thereafter. The plan of care must be developed within seven days of the assessment and reviewed every three months and whenever a resident's condition changes. Care planning conferences are required every three months or whenever a change occurs. As proxy, you should be notified of and attend these care conferences and advocate the principal's right to make decisions or exercise your responsibility as proxy if the principal is unable to do so. You should advocate all necessary rehabilitation therapy and other treatment that will enable the principal to function at the highest level of physical, mental, and social activity possible. The advance directive should be the basis for any medical treatment decisions such as resuscitation, tube feeding, or hospitalization for treatments not necessary for comfort. The Patient Self-Determination Act strengthens the power of the directive and of the proxy. You should insist that death be recognized and prepared for in the care plan; advocate hospice care within the nursing home and ask about the policies related to dying.

When Death Comes

Finally, if you must make a decision to withdraw life-sustaining treatment, ask for support. Ask other members of the family to be with you; ask the doctor, your or the patient's religious or spiritual advisor, friends, or the hospital or nursing home chaplain or social worker. A family prayer service has been published for this occasion.[2] It contains thoughtful advice for making decisions and following through on them.

Remember that you will make mistakes and will regret them. This is inevitable, a risk that accompanies serving as a proxy. Following a program on living wills that I had given for a senior citizens' group, an elderly woman drew me aside and said, "It's been 12 years since my sister died, and I still feel so guilty for what I put her through. She'd had a stroke and was in the hospital, and the doctor called me at home to ask if I wanted her resuscitated. I asked him what that meant and he said, 'If her heart stops or if she stops breathing, do you want us to try to keep her alive?' I said, 'Yes.' They did resuscitate her twice and she lived for another five days, but I feel so bad about what I put her through." I assured her that she had only done what most people would do if the question of resuscitation were presented in such a sudden fashion, that the doctor or someone should have discussed this with her in advance and explained about resuscitation and how it might affect her sister. I hope she felt somewhat reassured and that her guilt was relieved, but she had suffered with it for 12 years. These are awesome decisions, and we are only human; we can only do what we believe is best. Sometimes we make mistakes.

My mother was in a nursing home in her home town, which was several hours distant from both my brother's home and my home, and we lived several hours from one another. Neither of us was able to visit her as often as we felt we should, so when a bed opened in a fine nursing home in my brother's town, he phoned me to ask if we should consider moving Mom to that home. We consulted with our sister, who lived in another state, and all decided it would be best to transfer her. We were uncertain if we should get her permission or notify her in advance. She had congestive heart failure and high blood pressure and was increasingly confused as a result of many small strokes. In the past few years, whenever she was faced with a decision, she became very anxious. So we decided, on the basis of what was in her best interest, not to inform her of our decision prior to the day of the move. We discussed this with the social worker in her current nursing home, who agreed with us. It was the wrong decision! When we came to transfer her, she was in a lucid period and was both hurt and angry that she had not been involved in the decision. Ten minutes later she was confused again, saying that she had to return to her house, where she had not lived for six years, because she'd promised to help in voter registration—something she had not done for years. Even so, we were wrong in not giving her the opportunity to decide, regardless of our intent to avoid harm. She undoubtedly would have agreed to the transfer, because it meant that a family member could visit her every day. We violated her right to decide, however, and thereby violated her. The best interest principle should not be applied unless it is absolutely impossible to empower personal decisions or to exercise substituted judgment.

HELPING SOMEONE ELSE
TO PREPARE AN ADVANCE DIRECTIVE

People ask, "How can I get my mother (or father or grandparent) to make a living will?" My first response is, "You can only suggest it." My second question is, "Have you prepared your own advance directive?" Usually the answer is "No."

The decision to prepare a directive must be voluntary. Not only is coercion illegal but a directive prepared merely to please another may not reflect the wishes of the declarant. Furthermore, the motivation of the second person may be questionable or questioned. My father-in-law (who died at home, as related earlier) did not have a living will. Although we knew that he did not want to be hospitalized again or go to a nursing home, we would have felt more comfortable with written instructions. We were reluctant to suggest that he prepare a living will, however, because he frequently said, "I'm sorry that I'm such a bother—such a burden for you." We were concerned that if we suggested a living will, he would interpret it as our wanting him to die. Fortunately, he was mentally competent until he died, and he had a doctor who took time to discuss his feelings with him, as reflected by the No CPR order. We were not required to exercise substituted judgment for him.

This does not mean that you should not discuss the idea of an advance directive with an elderly person. Before doing so, however, be sure that you have accurate information and are prepared to answer the question, "Do *you* have a living will?" (And if you've not prepared one, "If you think they're so helpful, why haven't you made one for yourself?" This advice and caution also applies to staff members of hospitals, nursing homes, home health care, hospice care, and HMOs, which are required under the Patient Self-Determination Act to ask their patients and clients if they have advance directives. It applies to physicians and lawyers as well!)

The answer to a related question, "Can I prepare a living will for someone else?," depends on state law, on what you mean by "prepare," and on your motivation for doing so. The Texas Natural Death Act permits parents, a spouse, or a legal guardian to prepare a directive on behalf of a "qualified patient" who is under 18 years of age. A qualified patient is one in a terminal condition as certified in writing by two physicians. (Terminal condition is defined as an incurable condition in which life-sustaining treatment would only prolong the moment of death and death is imminent.) To my knowledge, only Texas has such a provision; the other state laws state that competent adults may prepare directives, implying, although not stating, that people who have been determined to be incompetent and minors cannot. Some living will laws specifically state that declarants who are unable to write can communicate their wishes to a witness who will then transcribe them. In some states living wills are available in Braille for people who are blind.

If you are asked to help some one prepare a directive, be very careful that the wishes stated are the declarant's, not yours. In this situation, it would be prudent to ask the person to complete the Values History first, or you could ask the questions as a guide for both of you. The Values History (included in the Appendix) is a helpful tool if you are a proxy or guardian for someone who is considered legally incompetent to complete a living will. It can stimulate a discussion with the person, and provide a guide for you.

Now we will put all this together and write a directive.

CHAPTER 6

WRITING AND DISTRIBUTING YOUR DIRECTIVE

Now we will put the pieces together. At this point you have an understanding of some of the basic ethical and legal issues on which advance directives are based; you've gotten information about your state's laws; and you know about the more common medical treatments used in terminal care. You have thought about the end of your life and the care and treatment you want and do not want. You have talked with your family and, perhaps, your doctor, lawyer, friends, minister, priest, or rabbi. You have selected someone to serve as proxy and have talked with this person about your wishes; he or she has agreed to serve as your surrogate decision maker when you can no longer make decisions for yourself. Even so, putting all this together in writing can be difficult. This is when many give up!

You can use the following outline to write down your wishes and instructions. Then you can either transfer them to your state's required or suggested form or to the generic form obtained from Choice in Dying, or you can write on the form, "See attached document of X-pages, which is a statement of my wishes and treatment instructions." The reason for such formal language is to assure that your entire directive will be placed in your medical record.

You can also complete a Medical Directive form and attach it to your advance directive. The Medical Directive was developed by Drs. Linda and Ezekiel Emanuel of the Division of Medical Ethics, Harvard Medical School. It lists a variety of medical situations and medical treatments. For each situation and each treatment, you can check whether you want, don't want, are unsure, or want the treatment tried but stopped if there is no clear improvement.[1] Examples of these situations and treatments are shown in the Appendix, where you will also find instructions for ordering the entire Medical Directive.

You can give instructions for your funeral, burial, or cremation in your advance directive if you wish. I chose to do this separately for two reasons. I want my entire family, not just my proxy, involved in making decisions about my memorial service; this is *their* ceremony, not mine. I have left several requests to guide them, however, including my wish to be cremated.

My second reason is a practical one: My advance directive is part of my medical record, which has gotten thicker and thicker through the years. I see no reason to add more to it, especially with information that does not pertain to medical treatment decisions.

Videotaping a living will has been suggested as a means of communicating your wishes. A written document is necessary for your medical record, but if you feel that videotaping would be helpful to your family or your proxy, do so. Such a visual document might add to their comfort and provide an additional memorial of you. You might also discuss your wishes regarding funeral and burial arrangements on the videotape.

OUTLINE FOR A LIVING WILL
(INSTRUCTIVE ADVANCE DIRECTIVE)

NAME AND ADDRESS:

I. GENERAL STATEMENT OF MY WISHES
Some examples of statements you might wish to make:
  A. I believe that death is part of life. I do not want to be held in this life
    1. When God calls me home.
    2. When this life has no more meaning for me.
    3. _____
  B. Life has meaning for me
    1. Until my heart stops beating.
    2. As long as I can communicate with others.
    3. As long as I can care for myself.
    4. As long as _____
  C. The most important values I hold are
    1. Life itself, regardless of its quality.
    2. Making my own decisions, being in controls, or
    3. My religious belief, especially _____

4. The memory that I leave with my loved ones.
5. My family's welfare. I believe my family is best served by
   a) Letting them decide what is best.
   b) Letting me die without prolonging my death with medical treatment that will not benefit me.
   c) _____

II. WISHES AND INSTRUCTIONS FOR CARE AND MEDICAL TREATMENT

The following are my wishes and instructions, made after thoughtful consideration of their consequences, to be carried out if I have an incurable or irreversible physical or mental condition and can no longer continue a meaningful life as described above and am unable to make decisions for myself.

A. I want
   1. Care and treatment, including rehabilitation therapies and related services, that will make it possible for me to take part in activities of daily living as long as possible.
   2. Pain control measures.
      a) I want pain medication even if it will shorten my life.
      b) I do not want so much pain medication that I cannot feel pain or other suffering or cannot communicate with others.
   3. Hospice care.
   4. Other _____
B. (Option 1) I have given much thought to medical treatment and have decided that I do not want the following treatments in the following situations:
   1. If I am in a persistent vegetative state or other form of permanent unconsciousness, I do not want medical treatment. I do not want my dying prolonged so that I become a burden to my family or others. I particularly do not want artificially administered nutrition or hydration, to be kept alive on a respirator, or to have cardiopulmonary resuscitation attempted on me.
   2. For conditions other than permanent unconsciousness, my physician, with consent of my proxy, may begin medical treatments other than artificially administered nutrition and hydration or cardiopulmonary resuscitation to see if the treatment will benefit me. By benefit, I mean that treatment will make it possible for me to take part in activities of daily living,

to eat and drink, to move about, and to communicate with others. If, within a short period (as determined by my proxy after consultation with my physician), there is no benefit to me, I instruct that the treatment be withdrawn.

I do not want artificially administered nutrition and hydration under any circumstances (except for treatment of a temporary condition in which I am unable to eat or drink, and then only for a short time).

I do not want cardiopulmonary respiration attempted if I have an incurable or irreversible condition.

3. Other treatments that I do not want if I have an incurable or irreversible condition and these treatments will only prolong my dying and not benefit me are

a) Kidney dialysis.

b) Blood transfusions.

c) Antibiotics unless necessary for comfort.

d) Chemotherapy.

e) Surgery of any kind.

f) Major surgery unless absolutely necessary for my comfort.

g) Minor surgery unless necessary for my comfort.

h) Diagnostic tests unless necessary for my comfort.

i) Other.

I do not want my proxy, my family, my physician, or other providers of care to feel that they have caused my death by carrying out my wishes. I know that their actions were taken out of respect for me.

B. (Option 2) I have given much thought to medical treatment and have decided that I do want the following treatments in the following situations:

4. If I am in a persistent vegetative state or other form of permanent unconsciousness, I want whatever treatment is necessary to keep me alive until my physician determines that death will occur within a short time (is imminent). Such treatment may include artificially administered nutrition and hydration. I do (do not) want cardiopulmonary resuscitation attempted.

5. For conditions other than permanent unconsciousness, I want all treatments that my physician and my proxy believe will extend my life or otherwise benefit me.

B. (Option 3) I want my physician and my proxy jointly to make decisions about medical treatment for me.

C. Instructions Regarding Hospitalization. If I am in a nursing home or receiving home health care, I (do) do not want to be transferred to a hospital for medical treatment that will only prolong my dying. I especially do not want to be sent to the hospital for the following treatments unless there are no alternatives to control pain:

  1. Antibiotics to treat pneumonia or other infections.

  2. Cardiopulmonary resuscitation.

  3. Mechanical respiration.

  4. Insertion of a feeding tube.

  5. Blood transfusions.

  6. Surgery, unless necessary for comfort.

  7. Chemotherapy.

  8. Diagnostic tests.

  9. Other.

D. Organ Donation. I do (do not) want my proxy to consent to the donation of my organs or other body parts after my death. (If you wish to donate your organs, the following statement will help your proxy: I understand that if my organs are to be donated, my body will be kept on a mechanical respirator until I am declared brain dead.)

E. Autopsy. I do (do not) want my proxy to consent to an autopsy of my body.

F. Disposition of Body.

  1. Name of mortuary.

  2. Burial in casket.

    a) Traditional funeral service or memorial service.

      (1) Location of service such as home, church, mortuary.

      (2) Other instructions regarding service.

    b) Open or closed casket.

    c) Burial instructions.

      (1) Private or not.

      (2) Cemetery or other location.

  3. Cremation

    a) Memorial service or not.

      (1) Instructions regarding service.

    b) Disposition of ashes.
      (1) Burial site.
      (2) Other instructions regarding ashes.
    c) Other instructions.

Note: If you use this as an attachment to your state's living will form or instead of another form, be sure to sign it and have it witnessed.

APPOINTING A PROXY

As recommended earlier, you should do this by designating a health care proxy in your living will and appointing an agent through a durable power of attorney for health care (DPAHC) or general durable power of attorney (DPA) form. Be sure to designate the same person in both forms. For a DPAHC or DPA, use the forms required or recommended by your state law (sources listed in Chapter 3), or contact your lawyer, the state bar association, or Choice in Dying. (See Resource section of the Appendix.) Your proxy must sign the DPAHC/DPA form, and even though some state living will laws do not require the proxy's signature on the living will, you should still have the proxy sign; it will indicate a commitment by the proxy. Attach the DPAHC/DPA form to your living will.

    If your living will form does not contain a proxy designation section, you should add the following to your written instructions:

> If I become unable to communicate my instructions, I designate _____ to act on my behalf, consistent with my instructions, as stated in my written directive. Unless I write instructions that limit my proxy's authority, my proxy has full power and authority to make health care decisions for me until and unless I revoke that authority. If a guardian or conservator of the person is to be appointed for me, I nominate my proxy, as named herein, to act as my guardian.

> If the person named above is unable or unavailable to act on my behalf, I authorize _____ to act as my proxy.[2]

Write or type in the names, addresses, and phone numbers of your proxy and alternate proxy, and ask each of them to sign the document. (This is another opportunity to examine the form and discuss your instructions with your proxy.) Attach the proxy designation to your living will.

SIGNING AND WITNESSING THE DIRECTIVE

The next step is to have your signature witnessed. Follow the instructions regarding witnesses in your state's living will and DPAHC/DPA laws. Sign both documents in the presence of the witnesses. If you plan to meet with your doctor in the near future, you could wait until after that meeting. Your doctor may advise some language changes, and if you decided to make those changes, you could avoid having to repeat the witnessing step. If you cannot meet with your doctor in the near future or you do not have a primary care physician, it would be prudent to have it witnessed immediately.

DISCUSSING YOUR DIRECTIVE WITH YOUR DOCTOR

This is one of the most important steps in the entire process, because your doctor is the one who must recommend treatment and write treatment orders. It would be helpful if your proxy could participate in this meeting as well. Bring your directive with you when you have your next regular appointment, or schedule one for this purpose. The goal is to ensure that medical decisions will be made collaboratively between you or your proxy and your doctor; trust must be established among all three parties.

If you did not meet with your doctor earlier in the process, it's possible that at this point, your doctor may suggest some changes, based on your medical condition. Ask the reasons for any changes, take time to think about your doctor's recommendations, and decide whether you want to incorporate them into your directive. (This is why it's best not to make copies and distribute them before visiting your doctor unless you do not have a doctor or are not able to discuss the directive soon after preparing it.) If your doctor accepts your directive as written, sign it in the presence of witnesses, make copies, and ask that a copy be put in your medical record in the doctor's or clinic's office. This does not mean that if you are admitted to a hospital, nursing home, home health program, or hospice, your medical record will follow you. You or your proxy should make sure that these other health care providers are given a copy when you are admitted for care and that it is placed in your medical record; the Patient Self-Determination Act is a reminder to them and to you.

For those of us who see a physician only once a year for a regular checkup, the advance directive may not seem relevant as long as we have no medical problems. It does have a purpose, however; its presence reminds our doctors that we have given thoughtful consideration to the end of our lives. This is especially important if you do not have one primary care physician. I belong to a health maintenance organization (HMO) and, although I usually can make an appointment with the same physician, occasionally there is physician turnover so my previous physician is not there or I decide to make an appointment with a gynecologist rather than a family practice physician or an internist. At each visit, I ask if my living will is in my medical record. It is, of course, but it's my way of reminding both of us of its presence, and the question usually evokes discussion of the topic. Only once did I find a physician unwilling to talk about it. He was so uncomfortable with my questions that I dropped the topic. He may not have known much about advance directives, or he may not have approved of them. Whatever the reason, I decided to select another physician.

As I grow older, I intend to seek out a physician knowledgeable about and interested in geriatric medicine and hope to establish an ongoing relationship with one physician. Many hospitals and medical groups have "seniors' clinics" that specialize in geriatric medicine. If you do not have a primary care physician, you might consider a seniors' clinic so that you can establish a relationship with one physician. This is the doctor with whom you should discuss your advance directive. If you do not have a primary care physician, your advance directive is even more important as a guide.

What if your physician refuses to discuss your advance directive or to accept it or has strong feelings in opposition to yours? Perhaps, as in Mrs. A's situation, the disagreement is about tube feeding. Under most living will laws, it is then your responsibility to decide whether to transfer to another doctor, if you are able to do so. In some states, the law requires physicians and other health care providers to assist the transfer if the patient is unable to do so. Hopefully, this situation can be averted by early thoughtful discussion with your physician.

DISTRIBUTING YOUR DIRECTIVE

Make a list of the people who should have copies of your directive: Your proxy, your doctor, plus any others whom you wish to have a copy. Make a copy for each plus several additional copies to bring to a hospital or nursing home, or to give to a home care or hospice nurse if needed. Keep the original yourself, and tell your proxy where you keep it so that more copies can be made as necessary. Do not put it in your safe deposit box, where it may be inaccessible when needed.

Your advance directive may be a multipage document. It will include the living will, plus any additional pages you have attached to it, and the durable power of attorney document. It may also include the Values History and the Medical Directive. Your proxy should have copies of the entire packet of documents, and you should show the entire packet to your doctor, who may advise that only the living will with any additional written instructions and your DPAHC or DPA agreement should be placed in your medical record at this time. All the documents should be readily available to your caregivers at the time the plan for terminal care is prepared. Be sure to keep the list of all who have copies of your directive, so that if you change or revoke it, you can notify each of them.

WHEN YOU TRAVEL OR MOVE TO ANOTHER STATE

When you travel, or if you spend part of the year in another state, be sure to take your directive with you. If you are hospitalized, the directive will notify the caregivers that you have selected a proxy and that you have thought about and formulated instructions for your treatment. Remember, though, that in an emergency, especially if you are far from home and among strangers, treatment may be started; the principle of implied consent will govern. After the emergency treatment, however, you or your proxy should have the right to consent to or refuse treatment.

If you move to another state, find out if that state's law requires a specific form. If it does not, your directive should be sufficient if it contains the elements described above. If a specific form is required for either a living will or a DPAHC, it would be wise to complete the required form. You may also wish to appoint another proxy if your original one is not readily available. If this state has restrictions, such as a narrow definition of terminal condition, or will not permit a person to refuse tube feeding, it is all the more important that you establish a relationship with a physician in your new community and explain your wishes. Again, you can contact a local hospital or the state hospital, medical, or bar association for information and advice.

SHOULD YOU REGISTER YOUR ADVANCE DIRECTIVE?

If you do not have a family or other proxy, if you travel to other states, or if you live in another state for part of the year, it might be useful to have your directive on file with an organization. This adds one more name to your list of people to contact if you change or cancel your directive.

Mississippi requires living wills to be registered with the State Department of Health and charges a registration fee; DPAHCs do not have to be registered. There may be a voluntary registry in your state—another question to ask when you gather information about your state's laws. You can also register your directive with Choice in Dying (see Resource section of the Appendix), which charges a one-time registration fee of $35 for members, $40 for nonmembers. Your directive will be reviewed to make sure that it is properly executed, and you will be given a wallet card with your registration number and a 24-hour registry telephone number.

If you do not travel frequently, your proxy is readily available, and your doctor is supportive of your directive, registration should not be necessary. Because of the PSDA, your directive will be in your medical record when you begin to receive care. Only you can make the decision to register or not, based on your own situation.

REVIEWING, REVISING, OR REVOKING YOUR ADVANCE DIRECTIVE

An advance directive is a living document; it is not cast in stone, never to be changed. You should review yours periodically to be sure that it continues to reflect your wishes about medical treatment and your designated proxy. As we mentioned earlier, a few states—California and Oregon (for a DPAHC) among them—require that directives be renewed periodically.

If you decide to change either your instructions or your proxy, it would be best to prepare a new directive. If you decide to revoke (cancel) your directive, you must notify your doctor and other health care providers who have copies. Do this in writing, if possible, although the laws say that you can notify them in any manner. Whether you change or revoke your directive, you should notify everyone who has a copy of your earlier directive and ask them either to destroy it or return it to you so you can destroy it.

All this may seem to be such a formidable an undertaking that your are overwhelmed. Do not be. Preparing an advance directive may seem much more difficult than preparing a property will or other financial directive, but both tasks are part of living. Once you have done it, you can be secure in the knowledge that you have taken the action necessary to face the end of life with as much assurance as possible. But do not undertake the preparation of either a medical or a financial directive in a hurry or at the last moment. Do not be persuaded to just "sign a living will," as a friend of mine was. She and her husband made an appointment with their lawyer to draw up their property will. After this was done, the lawyer asked them, "Have you made your living wills?" They had not, nor had they even talked about doing so. The lawyer asked, "Do you want to be kept alive on machines?" They looked at one another and decided they did not. The lawyer then produced some forms, and they signed them! Then they put them in their safe deposit box!

The Appendix contains a summary outline of the process for preparing an advance directive with references back to the page on which each step is discussed. You can use it as a checklist as you go through the steps. In Chapter 7, we'll discuss advance planning for some financial matters.

CHAPTER 7

SOME FINANCIAL CONSIDERATIONS

Two financial considerations that are especially important as we approach the "senior stage" of our lives are planning for the distribution of our property after death and paying for health care. Both are essential to our well being and to the well being of our families. Let's first consider how we can plan for distribution of our property.

PREPARING A FINANCIAL DIRECTIVE

Financial directives include documents stating how we want our financial assets distributed after we die, and appointing a financial proxy, someone to manage our financial affairs should we become unable to do so. The document that directs the distribution of financial assets can be a will, (last will and testament) or a trust. Making a financial (property) will is similar to making a living will in some ways; in others it's very different.

Financial directives differ from medical treatment directives in that state laws governing property and financial directives and disposition are more complicated than living will laws. The differences among states are even greater than they are for medical directives. Therefore, legal advice and assistance are essential if you are to achieve your goals for distribution of your property.

One similarity between medical and financial directives is that the majority of the people in our country have neither, reflecting a reluctance to think about death. A reason frequently given for not having a property will is, "My estate is so small that it would not pay for me to make out a will." This is a mistaken idea. It's especially important for people with modest estates to make out financial directives, because many of the costs associated with probate can be reduced or eliminated, making more money available to their heirs. Another reason given for not making out a will is, "The state will take care of it for me." The probate court will distribute your estate, but not necessarily in the manner that will be most beneficial to your survivors. Therefore, preparing a financial directive is a responsible act; it will benefit your survivors, and it can benefit you as well. The process for preparing a financial directive is similar to that for a medical directive.

Step One: Gather Information

The first step in preparing a financial directive is to learn about the various types of wills and trusts. You can get a general idea by reading some of the books listed in the Bibliography section of the Appendix. Read more than one so that you get several perspectives, several opinions.

There are several types of wills. *Attested* wills are the most common. There are also *holographic* (handwritten) wills, which are not legal in some states and restricted in others, and *pourover* wills, which are used with trusts. There are various types of living trusts: revocable and irrevocable living trusts, Q-tip trusts, life insurance trusts, and Medicaid Qualifying Trusts. Property ownership is equally complicated. Is your property in joint tenancy or tenancy-in-common, community property, or owned individually or by a partnership? What difference does it make? It makes a big difference, depending upon your state laws and your own situation. There are financial considerations such as probate costs, estate taxes, and attorney's fees.

Probate is the process used to distribute property after a person dies. You can tell the probate court through a will how you want your property distributed and name the person you select to carry out the distribution within the limits of state law. If you do not make out a will, the probate court will distribute your property according to the formula in your state's law and appoint someone to carry out the required tasks—for a fee. The costs of probate will be charged to your estate, and they could be much greater if you have not made a will and appointed a personal representative. There are also estate taxes, which can be avoided or reduced through advance planning.

A living trust makes it possible to settle an estate without a court procedure, and it may save estate taxes as well. You should consult a knowledgeable lawyer for advice on which type of trust is best suited to your situation. You will pay the cost of establishing the trust, which usually is more expensive than making out a will, but your heirs could be spared considerable expense in probate and estate taxes.

Before you consult with a lawyer, you should complete step two, which is similar to the second step in preparing a medical treatment directive. You must think about how you want your property distributed after you die or if you should become unable to manage your affairs. Who would you want to make financial decisions that would affect you and your family? The person you select for a health care proxy may not be the person you would choose to act as personal representative (executor) of your estate. Nor does the personal representative have as much discretion; probate laws limit the representative's authority. Your decision will be influenced by your stage in life. If you have minor children, their emotional and physical welfare, as well as their financial welfare, will be an important consideration. You might be advised to appoint a guardian for them until they reach the age of majority in your state, because the guardian can be given broader power than the personal representative.

Step Two: Inventory Your Possessions

The next step in preparing a financial directive is to make an inventory of all your possessions. You may already have such a list if you have applied for a home loan, for example. If not, you probably can get a form from your bank, an office supply store, or a local mortuary. We often overlook the mortuary as a source of information related to a variety of end-of-life matters.

You will need a list of both financial and personal information. By compiling a detailed list of such information in advance, you can save time in the lawyer's office. Remember, a lawyer's time is money. Not only will the list be useful to you and your lawyer as you make out your financial directives, but it will also help those who must make decisions after your death. Therefore, you might as well make the list as complete as possible now.

The type of information you will need is as follows:

Property and Financial Information
Write down the names, addresses, and phone numbers of the banks and other institutions that maintain each of the following, where the records are kept, the current amounts, and who to contact for each:

Money assets

1. Bank accounts—checking and savings.
2. Insurance policies—life, accident, homeowner, car, and health.

3. Pension information.
4. Deferred annuities/IRAs.
5. Investments.
6. Debts owed to you.

Liabilities

1. Credit card debt.
2. Personal loans other than real estate mortgages (including car).

Home and Other Real Property

1. Current market value and amount of remaining mortgage on your home.
2. Address, current market value, and amount of remaining mortgage on other real estate that you own or have an interest in.

Personal property

For large items that are licensed, such as boats and cars, list current value, outstanding debt, and where the title papers are located. You can itemize other personal property, such as furniture, clothing, and jewelry, or calculate the value and later make a directive stating your wishes about the disposal of these items. You may want to direct some as gifts, have everything sold and the proceeds distributed with the remainder of your estate, or provide for a combination of gifts and sale. Your lawyer will advise you regarding the law in your state.

Personal Information

1. Your social security number and location of your social security card.
2. Your birth date and date of marriage, location of birth certificate and marriage license. If you do not have a copy of your birth certificate or your marriage license, you can get a copy from the state registrar of vital statistics. You can phone a local hospital for the address and phone number.
3. Names, ages, and current addresses of your children. If you do not have children, list your closest relatives.

4. Location of military records, naturalization papers, and other special documents. If you do not have your military records, contact the state or regional Veterans Administration office.

5. Location of your personal address book or files. Although your lawyer will not need this information, it will be of immeasurable help to those who plan your funeral and take over your correspondence.

6. Income tax information, including past returns and current estimated tax payments and records.

7. Name, address, and phone number of the funeral home of your choice. If you belong to a memorial society or a cremation association, write down the address and phone number. You can include your funeral and burial wishes in this document, in your living will, or in a separate document.

8. Location of safe deposit box and keys. Be sure that your personal representative's name and signature are on the safe deposit access list.

9. Lawyer's name, address, and phone number.

Step Three: Consult an Attorney

I strongly advise consulting a lawyer for assistance in preparing your financial directive so that you can make the type of directive that will provide you with maximum benefit. It is important to select a lawyer who is knowledgeable in probate law. My husband and I were fortunate in that a lawyer friend, who is not a probate lawyer, recommended a colleague who is very knowledgeable. We trusted his advice and are quite satisfied with the results. This lawyer took time to ask about our goals for property distribution and suggested several ways we could meet those goals. You can ask your state bar association (see Resource section of the Appendix) for a list of probate lawyers, and you can ask friends about their experiences. Be sure to ask what the fees will be before making a final decision on a lawyer.

After receiving your lawyer's advice, you may want to proceed directly with preparation of your will or trust, or you may want to think about it for a while. Do not be rushed. You may want to discuss the options with your family, especially with the person you will ask to serve as your personal representative, if you prepare a will, or your trustee, if you decide on a living trust. The process of selecting your representative or trustee is similar to that of selecting a health care proxy, although you may be looking for different qualities in each. You do not need to name the same person for both tasks; in fact, it may not be advisable. Only you can decide.

If you decide on a living trust, you can save legal fees by transferring your assets into the trust yourself, but it will take some time and effort. You must contact each entity identified above—banks, investment houses, insurance companies, pension plans—and have each account transferred to your trust. Your lawyer can advise you how to do this. Your lawyer can do it for you, but you will pay for the service.

Step Four: Distribute Copies of Your Financial Directive

Your lawyer may advise you to file your will or trust document with a county probate court, where it will be accessible only to you. After your death, your personal representative will be able to retrieve it. There is mixed opinion as to whether to keep the document in a safe deposit box because it might be difficult for your representative to retrieve it. You should ask your lawyer or the bank where you have your safe deposit box about the law and practice in your state.

I believe that your heirs should know the provisions of your will or trust. By discussing it with them in advance, just as with a medical treatment directive, you will prepare them for the future, for the time when you are not here. It is one of the steps in preparing for the great journey and for those we leave behind.

FINANCIAL DURABLE POWER OF ATTORNEY

Just as it is important to have a health care proxy in addition to a living will, it is important to have a financial proxy as well as a last will and testament or a living trust.

You can appoint a financial proxy, called an *attorney-in-fact* under the Durable Power of Attorney (DPA) law of your state. DPA laws were enacted by all the states before any states passed Durable Power of Attorney for Health Care (DPAHC) laws. (You may recall that we said earlier that if you live in a state that does not have a DPAHC law, you should appoint a health care attorney-in-fact using a DPA form.) The purpose of appointing either a financial or health care attorney-in-fact is to have someone you trust make decisions for you when you are unable to make them. In medical practice, the next of kin is usually accepted as decision maker for an incompetent person, but this is not true for financial matters. Banks require a legal document before they allow a person other than the account holder to cash checks, for example. Therefore, it is prudent to appoint another person to act as your financial attorney-in-fact if you become unable to manage your affairs. The alternative is legal guardianship, which can be time-consuming and expensive to obtain, and gives you no control over who the court will appoint as guardian. You should exercise as much thought and care in selecting your financial attorney-in-fact (who does not have to be a lawyer and usually is a family member) as you would in selecting a health care proxy, because there is no court oversight with DPA as there is with guardianship.

PAYING FOR HEALTH CARE IN THE LATER YEARS OF LIFE

For many people, the time when they need more medical care comes at a time when they have fixed incomes and less money to pay for care or for health insurance. Medicare is the government-sponsored health insurance program for people 65 years and older who are not covered by another federal retirement program.

Medicare

There are two payment programs under Medicare. Part A pays for inpatient hospital care, including hospital psychiatric care, home health care, hospice care, and a limited amount of nursing home care. Medicare Part B pays medical (physician) costs. You do not have to have a physical examination or other test to qualify for Medicare. People who are receiving social security benefits at age 65 will be notified automatically that they are enrolled in Part A; they will be enrolled in Part B unless they notify the Social Security Administration that they do not want it. The monthly fee for Part B is deducted from the monthly social security benefit check; in 1992 the monthly fee was $31.80. People not receiving social security benefits at age 65 must apply for Medicare coverage, so if you are 65 and are not receiving monthly social security payments, contact the social security office in your state. The number is in the phone book under federal government offices, or you can phone your library or the state ombudsman's office. (See Resource section in the Appendix.) If you are still working and are covered by health insurance, be sure to find out from your personnel office what coverage your employer will provide in addition to Medicare.

Additional Health Insurance: Medigap Policies

Medicare does not pay all the costs of health care; there are large gaps in the coverage. In 1992 you would pay $652 on the first admission to a hospital in each benefit period. A benefit period begins on the day you enter a hospital and continues until you have been out of the hospital or a skilled nursing home for 60 days. Medicare pays the remainder of all hospital charges and skilled nursing care for 60 days. You would pay $163 as copayment for days 61 through 90. After day 90 you would begin using up your 60 *lifetime reserve* days, for which you pay a $326 (1992) copayment per day. In addition to the deductible and copayments, there are other charges that Medicare does not pay, nor does it pay for care received outside of the United States, except under limited circumstances in Canada and Mexico.

There are similar gaps in the Part B medical coverage. In 1992 these included a $100 annual deductible and 20% coinsurance for additional costs. In addition, if your doctor's charges are greater than those approved by Medicare, you must pay the additional charges, unless your doctor is a Medicare Participating Physician. So you should find out if your doctor, or a doctor you may be considering, participates in Medicare. There are other exclusions in Part B. It does not pay for most prescription drugs, eye examinations, glasses, hearing aids, dental care, or routine physicals.

As for nursing home care, Medicare pays only for skilled nursing care provided in a skilled nursing facility that is Medicare approved. Your doctor must certify that skilled nursing care is needed. To qualify, you must have been in a hospital for at least three days and enter the nursing home within 30 days of discharge from the hospital. My mother-in-law was discharged from the hospital directly to the nursing home on the third day, a relatively common practice. We did not know that she had an infection at the time of discharge. She was transferred back to the hospital emergency room within 48 hours, in the middle of the night, for intravenous antibiotics, and my father-in-law had to pay several hundred dollars in ambulance charges. Had we known about the infection, we would have insisted that she stay at the hospital for treatment until the infection was under control. You have the right to appeal a discharge, but it may take assertive advocacy to be heard. The hospital patient representative is the person to contact. (You can also appeal Medicare payment decisions, but be prepared to cope with several layers of bureaucracy from the local insurance company that serves as a Medicare carrier on up to the federal Health Care Financing Administration.)

Other gaps in Medicare's nursing home benefits are that after the first 20 days, which are paid in full, the copayment is $81.50 (1992) per day through day 100, at which time coverage ends. There are also gaps in home health care and in hospice care, although not as many for hospice.

You will need supplemental health insurance unless you are prepared to pay these additional costs yourself. Many employers will pay all or part of the premiums for supplemental insurance for retired employees, so first check with your employer's personnel office. If your employer does not provide this benefit or if you have to choose between several plans, find out about the benefits and costs of each. Under a new federal law, effective August 1, 1992, states must require insurance companies to offer standardized Medigap policies. There are 10 different packages of benefits, which range from basic Package A to Package J. J not only pays the basic benefits of supplemental coverage for Parts A and B plus the first three pints of blood but pays the deductible for Parts A and B, the skilled nursing home copayment, foreign travel emergency, at-home recovery, excess physician charges, preventive care, and outpatient prescription drugs. The premiums, of course, are higher for the packages that offer more benefits. States are not required to insist that all 10 benefit policies be made available. Three states—Masssachusetts, Minnesota, and Wisconsin—which already require core Medigap benefits plus standard riders, are not required to offer the standard benefit policies.[1]

A new Medicare supplemental insurance called Medicare Select was being tested in 16 states in 1992 and may be expanded to other states. These policies require enrollees, in exchange for a lower premium, to use a *preferred provider* selected by the insurance company.[2] For those who already belong to an HMO, this may not make a difference; those who have a long-standing relationship with a physician who is not on the preferred provider list might have to transfer to another physician or pay the costs themselves.

The federal Health Care Financing Agency publishes several guides on Medicare and Medigap, and your state's department of insurance should be able to provide information, as should the state long-term care ombudsman's office. Addresses and phone numbers of additional agencies are included in the Resource section.

Medicaid

Medicaid is a state administered program, funded in part by federal dollars, that pays for health care for low income people . In some states, Medicaid pays the Medigap costs for low income elderly people and for nursing home care for people who are indigent, many of whose own resources have been used up paying for nursing home care. The states set standards for the income and other assets a person must have to qualify for Medicaid assistance.

The Qualified Medicare Beneficiary (QMB) Program is designed to assist people who cannot afford a Medigap policy. If your income is below $6,800 ($9,200 for a couple), Medicaid may pay your Medicare Part B premium and provide additional supplemental coverage.

To find out if you or the person for whom you are a proxy qualifies for Medicaid, ask a hospital or nursing home social worker, the state health or human services department, or the long-term care ombudsman. (See Resource section in the Appendix.)

Long-Term Care (Nursing Home) Insurance

In addition to those standardized Medigap policies that cover skilled nursing home copayments, some insurance companies offer insurance designed to pay some of the costs of nursing home care. The premiums are expensive, however, unless you subscribe at a relatively young age, so it's important to consider the "opportunity costs"—the alternate uses for the premium money. My father-in-law took out nursing home insurance for his wife and himself at age 84. He did not recoup the amount of money he paid in premiums for the six months that his wife was in the nursing home. Had she lived six months longer, the reimbursement for care would have approximately equaled the amount of the premiums. Had he put that money in an interest-bearing account during those same years, he would have had more money. But had he needed nursing home care, the insurance benefits would have exceeded the premium cost, so you must consider many factors in making a decision. There may be a limit on the total amount that the policy will pay. Do not buy any nursing home insurance without first checking out the company and the policy with your state department of insurance or the long-term care ombudsman's office. (See Resources section in the Appendix.)

And so we end this book on the theme that has guided us through each chapter: It is your responsibility to make the decision. There are many resources to assist you, but the final choice is yours.

END NOTES

CHAPTER 1

1. J. Gordon Melton, *The Churches Speak On: Euthanasia* (Detroit: Gale Research, 1991), pp. 141 and 157.
2. Steven H. Miles, "Informed Demand for 'Non-Beneficial' Medical Treatment," *NEJM* 325, no. 7, pp. 512-515.
3. *In re the Conservatorship of Helga M. Wanglie,* Minnesota District Court, Hennepin County Probate Division, File No. PX–91–283.
4. Paul Homer and Martha Holsted, *A Good Old Age? The Paradox of Setting Limits* (New York: Simon & Schuster, 1990), p. 25.
5. E. Van Allen and D. Gay Moldow, "The Case of Helga Wanglie," *Ethics News* 10 (Spring 1991).
6. Lawrence J. Schneiderman, et al., "Effects of Offering Advance Directives on Medical Treatment and Costs," *AnnInMed* 117 (October 1, 1992), pp. 599–606.
7. Ibid.
8. Arthur Caplan, "Living Wills Might Not Make a Difference, Study Finds," *St. Paul Pioneer Press,* October 12, 1992.

CHAPTER 2

1. "Draft Guidelines for State Court Decision Making in Authorizing or Withholding Life-Sustaining Medical Treatment, 1991," (Richmond, Va.: National Center for State Courts), (Final version, September 1992.)
2. Different terms are used for guardianship in different states. For example, some use *conservatorship* to denote a limited form of guardianship, and some use *special guardianship.* The process is similar in all states, however.

CHAPTER 3

1. *In re Guardianship of Browning,* No. 74, 134, Florida Supreme Court, 13 September 1990.

2. Arnold R. Beisser, *A Graceful Passage: Notes on the Freedom to Live or Die* (New York: Bantam Books, 1991), p. 147.

CHAPTER 4

1. "Life-Sustaining Technologies and the Elderly," Publication BA 306 (Washington, D.C.: Office of Technology Assessment, 1989).

2. David Scheidermayer, "The Decision to Forgo CPR in the Elderly Patient," *JAMA* 260, no. 14, pp. 2096–2097. And Donald Murphy, "Do-Not-Resuscitate Orders: Time for Reappraisal in Long-Term Care Institutions," *JAMA* 260, no. 14, pp. 2098–2101.

3. *Brophy* v. *New England Sinai Hospital, Inc.* Massachusetts Supreme Judicial Court, 393 Mass. 417. N.E. 22d 626, (1986).

4. *Nancy Beth Cruzan, Her Parents and Co-Guardians, Lester L. Cruzan* v. *Director, Missouri Dept. of Health, et al.* U.S. Supreme Court, 496 U.S. 110 S.Ct. 2841, 1111. Ed. 2d (1990).

5. American Medical Association, Council on Ethical and Judicial Affairs, "Statement on Withholding or Withdrawing Life Prolonging Treatment," March 15, 1986.

6. Giles R. Scofield, "Artificial Feeding· The Least Restrictive Alternative?" *JAGS* 39, no. 12, pp. 1217–20

7. Ibid, pp. 1217 and 1219.

8. This aspect of the case raises questions about informed consent. If this woman was so depressed as to need electric shock treatments, was she competent to consent to the treatment? Could this be considered an emergency? She had no family or proxy to give consent, so who should do so? The treatments apparently benefited her, so was the doctor, acting on the principle of best interest, carrying out his ethical duty to a patient?

9. The Medical Decisions Advocate Project was a pilot project designed to provide specially trained advocates for people without family or friends for whom an urgent medical decision is needed. Its purpose was to provide an alternative to legal guardianship. The project was funded by the Institute of Public Law, University of New Mexico, under a grant from an anonymous donor. For more information, contact Joan Gibson, Ph.D., Project Director, National Medical Guardianship Project, Center for Health Law and Ethics, Institute of Public Law, University of New Mexico, 111 Stanford NE, Albuquerque, NM 87141, 505/277-5006.

10. *Cruzan* v. *Director, Missouri Dept. of Health* (1990).

11. John Ely, Philip Peters, Steven Zweig, Nancy Elder, and F. David Schneider, "The Physician's Decision to Use Tube Feeding: The Role of the Family, the Living Will, and the Cruzan Decision," *JAGS* 40, no. 5, pp. 471–475.

12. *In re Quinlan,* New Jersey Supreme Court, 70 N.J. 10, 355A. 2d 647 (1976).

13. Sandal Stoddard, *The Hospice Movement,* (Briarcliff Manor, N.Y.: Stein and Day, 1978).

14. The Hennepin County Medical Society convened a task force to develop guidelines for the use of morphine and other pain relief measures for dying patients. The resulting guidelines emphasized the duty of physicians to ease the pain of dying patients, even though this might hasten death. The welfare of the patient must be the primary concern. These guidelines cited the principle of double effect. ("Guidelines for the Management of Pain and Suffering of Dying Persons," (Minneapolis: Hennepin County Medical Society, 1991).)

CHAPTER 5

1. *Elbaum* v. *Grace Plaza of Great Neck.* New York Supreme Court, Appellate Division. 148 A.D. 2d 244, 544 N.Y. S. 2d, 1989.

2. Thomas A. Shannon and Charles N. Faso, *Let Them Go Free; Family Prayer Service to Assist in the Withdrawal of Life Support* (Kansas City, Mo.: Sheed and Ward, 1985).

CHAPTER 6

1. Linda and Ezekiel Emanuel, "The Medical Directive: A New Comprehensive Advance Care Document," *JAMA* 261, pp. 3288–3293. And Linda Emanuel, "The Health Care Directive: Learning How to Draft Advance Care Documents," *JAGS* 39, no. 12, pp. 1221–1228.

2. From the Minnesota Living Will Act, Minn. Statute 145B.04.

CHAPTER 7

1. Michael Leonetti, "Understanding the New Medigap Insurance Alternatives," *AAIIJ* XIV, no. 8 (September 1992), pp. 26–28.

2.   National Association of Insurance Commissioners and the Health Care Financing Administration, U.S. Dept. of Health and Human Services, *1992 Guide to Health Insurance for People with Medicare.* (Washington, D.C.: U.S. Government Printing Office, 1992).

APPENDIXES

APPENDIX A

CHECKLIST FOR PREPARING AN ADVANCE DIRECTIVE

Begin the process early in life. Do not wait until you are admitted to a hospital or nursing home with a terminal illness.

Step One: Gather information about your state's law. (See Chapter 3 and Appendix E: Resources.) Questions to ask:

1. Do I have to use a special form for a living will? If the answer is yes, ask where you can get the form.
2. Can I appoint a health care proxy in my living will?
3. Is there a durable power of attorney for health care law?
4. Are there any restrictions on who can be a proxy or an attorney-in-fact?
5. Are there any restrictions on who can witness my directive?
6. When will my directive go into effect? When does it become operational?
7. How is terminal condition defined in the law?
8. Are there any kinds of medical treatment that I cannot refuse?
9. Can I refuse artificially administered nutrition and hydration (tube feeding)?
10. Am I required to register my directive with the state?
11. Is this information current? Does it include the most recent amendments to the law?

Step Two: Choose the type of directive (Chapter 3). Both a living will and a durable power of attorney agreement are recommended.

Step Three: Think about the end of life (Chapter 3).

1. Personal values, religious beliefs, and personal experiences.
2. Complete Values History (Appendix B).
3. Think about medical conditions and treatments that you want or do not want (Chapter 4) and the Medical Directive (Appendix C). Some questions to ask yourself and your doctor:
   - What kind of serious conditions can I expect?
   - What kind of treatment might be used for that condition?
   - What are the chances that the treatment would benefit me?
   - What do I mean by benefit?
   - What would happen if treatment did not benefit me?
   - What are the costs?
4. Read The Patient's Choice of Treatment Options (Appendix D).

Step Four: Talk with family, prospective proxy, doctor, and others about your thoughts and wishes (Chapter 3).

Step Five: Record your wishes on the form required in your state or a generic form, or create a document written or typed by you. If you decide to create your own document, attach it to the state form on which you have written, "See attached X-page statement of my wishes and instructions" (Chapter 6).

Step Six: Discuss the directive with your selected proxy and get proxy's consent to serve (Chapter 5).

Step Seven: Discuss your directive with your doctor (Chapters 4 and 6). Try to cover the following in your discussion.
1. Philosophy.
   - What are your feelings about and experiences with advance directives?
   - What do you consider a terminal condition?
   - What are your feelings about and experiences with hospice care?
2. Cardiopulmonary resuscitation.
   - Do you write do-not-resuscitate (DNR) orders?
   - At what point would you write a DNR order for me?
   - Would you discuss the chances of resuscitation with me or my proxy before writing a DNR order?

- Does our state or community have a policy about honoring DNR orders in the home? Would you write a DNR order for me if I were not in a hospital or nursing home?
- Would you withdraw a respirator if I were placed on one in a medical emergency and there was no hope for my recovery?

3. Tube feeding.
    - Would you honor my wish not to have tube feeding if there was no hope for my recovery?
    - Would you withdraw a feeding tube if I were placed on one and there was no hope for my recovery?

4. Additional question: What are your feelings about and experiences with hospice care?

Step Eight: Sign your directives (living will and durable power of attorney agreement) in the presence of witnesses (Chapter 6).

Step Nine: Copy and distribute your directive. Keep a list of all to whom you give copies. Keep the original in a safe place where it is readily accessible. Decide if you want to register it (Chapter 6).

Step Ten: Review, revise, and revoke if you change your mind (Chapter 6).

Step Eleven: Live life to the fullest, now that you have prepared for death.

APPENDIX B

The University of New Mexico

Center for Health Law and Ethics
Institute of Public Law
School of Law
1117 Stanford NE
Albuquerque, NM 87131-1446
Telephone (505) 277-5006
FAX (505) 277-7064

VALUES HISTORY FORM

NAME: _____

DATE: _____

If someone assisted you in completing this form, please fill in his or her name, address, and relationship to you.

Name: _____

Address: _____

_____

Relationship: _____

The purpose of this form is to assist you in thinking about and writing down what is important to you about your health. If you should at some time become unable to make health care decisions for yourself, your thoughts as expressed on this form may help others make a decision for you in accordance with what you would have chosen.

The first section of this form asks whether you have already expressed your wishes concerning medical treatment through either written or oral communications and if not, whether you would like to do so now. The second section of this form provides an opportunity for you to discuss your values, wishes, and preferences in a number of different areas, such as your personal relationships, your overall attitude toward life, and your thoughts about illness.

This form is not copyrighted; you may make as many copies as you wish.

103

SECTION 1

A. WRITTEN LEGAL DOCUMENTS

Have you written any of the following
legal documents? _____

If so, please complete the requested
information.

Living Will
Date written: _____
Document location: _____
Comments: (e.g., any limitations, special
requests, etc.) _____
_____
_____
_____

Durable Power of Attorney
Date written: _____
Document location: _____
Comments: (e.g., whom have you named
to be your decision maker?)
_____
_____
_____

**Durable Power of Attorney for Health
Care Decisions**
Date written: _____
Document location: _____
Comments: (e.g., whom have you named
to be your decision maker?)
_____
_____
_____

Organ Donations
Date written: _____
Document location: _____
Comments: (e.g., any limitations on which
organs you would like to donate?)
_____
_____
_____

B. WISHES CONCERNING SPECIFIC MEDICAL PROCEDURES

If you have ever expressed your
wishes, either written or orally,
concerning any of the following
medical procedures, please complete
the requested information. If you have
not previously indicated your wishes
on these procedures and would like to
do so now, please complete this
information.

Organ Donation
To whom expressed: _____
If oral, when? _____
If written, when? _____
Document location: _____
Comments: _____
_____
_____
_____
_____

Kidney Dialysis
To whom expressed: _____
If oral, when? _____
If written, when? _____
Document location: _____
Comments: _____
_____
_____
_____
_____

Cardiopulmonary Resuscitation (CPR)
To whom expressed: _____
If oral, when? _____
If written, when? _____
Document location: _____
Comments: _____
_____
_____
_____
_____

Respirators

To whom expressed: _____

If oral, when? _____

If written, when? _____

Document location: _____

Comments: _____

_____

_____

_____

Artificial Nutrition

To whom expressed: _____

If oral, when? _____

If written, when? _____

Document location: _____

Comments: _____

_____

_____

_____

Artificial hydration

To whom expressed: _____

If oral, when? _____

If written, when? _____

Document location: _____

Comments: _____

_____

_____

_____

C. GENERAL COMMENTS

Do you wish to make any general comments about the information you provided in this section? _____

_____

_____

_____

_____

SECTION 2

A. YOUR OVERALL ATTITUDE TOWARD YOUR HEALTH

1. How would you describe your current health status? If you currently have any medical problems, how would you describe them? _____

_____

_____

2. If you have current medical problems, in what ways, if any, do they affect your ability to function? _____

_____

3. How do you feel about your current health status? _____

_____

_____

4. How well are you able to meet the basic necessities of life--eating, food preparation, sleeping, personal hygiene, etc.? _____

_____

5. Do you wish to make any general comments about your overall health? _____

_____

_____

B. YOUR PERCEPTION OF THE ROLE OF YOUR DOCTOR AND OTHER HEALTH CAREGIVERS

1. Do you like your doctors? _____

2. Do you trust your doctors? _____

_____

3. Do you think your doctors should make the final decision concerning any treatment you might need? _____

_____

4. How do you relate to your caregivers, including nurses, therapists, chaplains, social workers, etc.? _____

_____

5. Do you wish to make any general comments about your doctor and other health caregivers? _____

_____
_____
_____

C. YOUR THOUGHTS ABOUT INDEPENDENCE AND CONTROL

1. How important is independence and self-sufficiency in your life? _____

_____

2. If you were to experience decreased physical and mental abilities, how would that affect your attitude toward independence and self-sufficiency? _____

_____

3. Do you wish to make any general comments about the value of independence and control in your life?

_____
_____
_____

D. YOUR PERSONAL RELATIONSHIPS

1. Do you expect that your friends, family and/or others will support your decisions regarding medical treatment you may need now or in the future? _____

_____
_____

2. Have you made any arrangements for your family or friends to make medical treatment decisions on your behalf? If so, who has agreed to make decisions for you and in what circumstances? _____

_____
_____

3. What, if any, unfinished business from the past are you concerned about (e.g., personal and family relationships, business and legal matters)? _____

_____
_____

4. What role do your friends and family play in your life? _____

_____
_____

5. Do you wish to make any general comments about the personal relationships in your life? _____

_____
_____

E. YOUR OVERALL ATTITUDE TOWARD LIFE

1. What activities do you enjoy (e.g., hobbies, watching TV, etc.)? _____

_____

2. Are you happy to be alive? _____

_____

3. Do you feel that life is worth living?

_____

4. How satisfied are you with what you have achieved in your life? _____

_____

_____

_____

5. What makes you laugh/cry? _____

_____

_____

_____

6. What do you fear most? What frightens or upsets you? _____

_____

_____

_____

7. What goals do you have for the future? _____

_____

_____

8. Do you wish to make any general comments about your attitude toward life?

_____

_____

_____

_____

F. YOUR ATTITUDE TOWARD ILLNESS, DYING, AND DEATH

1. What will be important to you when you are dying (e.g., physical comfort, no pain, family members present, etc.)? _____

_____

_____

2. Where would you prefer to die?

_____

_____

3. What is your attitude toward death? _____

_____

_____

_____

4. How do you feel about the use of life-sustaining measures in the face of: terminal illness? _____

permanent coma? _____

irreversible chronic illness (e.g., Alzheimer's disease)? _____

_____

5. Do you wish to make any general comments about your attitude toward illness, dying, and death? _____

_____

_____

G. YOUR RELIGIOUS BACKGROUND AND BELIEFS

1. What is your religious background? _____

_____

_____

2. How do your religious beliefs affect your attitude toward serious or terminal illness? _____

_____

_____

_____

3. Does your attitude toward death find support in your religion? _____

_____

4. How does your faith community, church or synagogue view the role of prayer or religious sacraments in an illness? _____

_____

_____

5. Do you wish to make any general comments about your religious background and beliefs? _____

_____

_____

_____

H. YOUR LIVING ENVIRONMENT

1. What has been your living situation over the last 10 years (e.g., lived alone, lived with others, etc.)? _____

_____

2. How difficult is it for you to maintain the kind of environment for yourself that you find comfortable? Does any illness or medical problem you have now mean that it will be harder in the future? _____

_____

_____

_____

3. Do you wish to make any general comments about your living environment?

_____

_____

_____

_____

I. YOUR ATTITUDE CONCERNING FINANCES

1. How much do you worry abut having enough money to provide for your care? _____

_____

_____

2. Would you prefer to spend less money on your care so that more money can be saved for the benefit of your relatives and/or friends? _____

_____

_____

_____

3. Do you wish to make any general comments concerning your finances and the cost of health care? _____

_____

_____

_____

_____

J. YOUR WISHES CONCERNING YOUR FUNERAL

1. What are your wishes concerning your funeral and burial or cremation?

_____

_____

_____

_____

_____

_____

2. Have you made your funeral arrangements? If so, with whom? _____

_____

_____

_____

3. Do you wish to make any general comments about how you would like your funeral and burial or cremation to be arranged or conducted? _____

_____

_____

_____

OPTIONAL QUESTIONS

1. How would you like your obituary (announcement of your death) to read?

_____
_____
_____
_____
_____
_____
_____
_____
_____
_____
_____

2. Write yourself a brief eulogy (a statement about yourself to be read at your funeral). _____

_____
_____
_____
_____
_____
_____
_____
_____
_____
_____
_____

SUGGESTIONS FOR USE

After you have completed this form, you may wish to provide copies to your doctors and other health caregivers, your family, your friends, and your attorney. If you have a Living Will or Durable Power of Attorney for Health Care Decisions, you may wish to attach a copy of this form to those documents.

Joan McIves Gibson, Ph.D., Center for Health, Law and Ethics, Institute of Public Law, The University of New Mexico, Albuquerque. Used with permission.

APPENDIX C

The Medical Directive

Introduction. As part of a person's right to self-determination, every adult may accept or refuse any recommended medical treatment. This is relatively easy when people are well and can speak. Unfortunately, during serious illness they are often unconscious or otherwise unable to communicate their wishes — at the very time when many critical decisions need to be made.

The Medical Directive allows you to record your wishes regarding various types of medical treatment in several representative situations so that your desires can be respected. It also lets you appoint someone to make medical decisions for you if you should you become unable to make them on your own.

The Medical Directive comes into effect only if you become incompetent (unable to make decisions or to express your wishes), and you can change it at any time until then. As long as you are competent, you should discuss your care directly with your physician.

Completing the Form. You should, if possible, complete the form in the context of a discussion with your physician. Ideally, this should occur in the presence of your proxy. This lets your physician and your proxy know how you think about these decisions, and it provides you and your physician with the opportunity to give or clarify relevant personal or medical information. You may wish to discuss the issues with your family, friends, or religious mentor.

The Medical Directive contains six illness situations that include incompetence. For each one, you consider possible interventions and goals of medical care. Situations A and B involve coma; C and D, dementia; E, chronic disability; E and F, temporary inability to make decisions.

The interventions are divided into six groups: 1) cardiopulmonary resuscitation or major surgery; 2) mechanical breathing or dialysis; 3) blood transfusions or blood products; 4) artificial nutrition and hydration; 5) simple diagnostic tests or antibiotics; and 6) pain medications, even if they dull consciousness and indirectly shorten life. Most of these treatments are described briefly. If you have further questions, consult your physician.

Your wishes for treatment options (I want this treatment; I want this treatment tried, but stopped if there is no clear improvement; I am undecided; I do not want this treatment) should be indicated. If you choose a trial of treatment, you should understand that this indicates you want the treatment *withdrawn* if your physician and proxy believe you would have agreed that it has become futile.

The Personal Statement section allows you to mention anything that you consider important to tell those who may make decisions for you concerning the limits of your life and the goals of intervention. For example, your description of insufferable disability in the Personal Statement will aid your health-care team in understanding exactly when to avoid interventions you may have declined in situation E. Or if, in situation B, you wish to define "uncertain chance" with numerical probability, you may do so here.

Next you may express your preferences concerning organ donation. Do you wish to donate your body or some or all of your organs after your death? If so, for what purpose(s) and to which physician or institution? If not, this should also be indicated in the appropriate box.

In the final section you may designate one or more proxy decision-makers, who would be asked to make choices under circumstances in which your wishes are unclear. You can indicate whether the decisions of the proxy should override, or be overridden by, your wishes if there are differences. And, should you name more than one proxy, you can state who is to have the final say if there is disagreement. Your proxy must understand that this role usually involves making judgments that you would have made for yourself, had you been able — and making them by the criteria you have outlined. Proxy decisions should ideally be made in discussion with your family, friends, and physician.

What to Do with the Form. Once you have completed the form, you and two adult witnesses (other than your proxy) who have no interest in your estate need to sign and date it.

Many states have legislation covering documents of this sort. To determine the laws in your state, you should call the office of its attorney general or consult a lawyer. If your state has a statutory document, you may wish to use the Medical Directive and append it to this form.

You should give a copy of the completed document to your physician. His or her signature is desirable but not mandatory. The Directive should be placed in your medical records and flagged so that anyone who might be involved in your care can be aware of its presence. Your proxy, a family member, and/or a friend should also have a copy. In addition, you may want to carry a wallet card noting that you have such a document and where it can be found.

Copyright 1990 by Linda L. Emanuel and Ezekiel J. Emanuel.

An earlier version of this form was originally published as part of an article by Linda L. Emanuel and Ezekiel J. Emanuel, "The Medical Directive: A New Comprehensive Advance Care Document," *Journal of the American Medical Association* 261:3288–3293, June 9, 1989. It does not reflect the official policy of the American Medical Association.

MY MEDICAL DIRECTIVE

This Medical Directive expresses, and shall stand for, my wishes regarding medical treatments in the event that illness should make me unable to communicate them directly. I make this Directive, being 18 years or more of age, of sound mind, and appreciating the consequences of my decisions.

1. Cardiopulmonary resuscitation (chest compressions, drugs, electric shocks, and artificial breathing aimed at reviving a person who is on the point of dying), **or major surgery** (for example, removing the gall bladder or part of the colon)

2. Mechanical breathing (respiration by machine, through a tube in the throat), **or dialysis** (cleaning the blood by machine or by fluid passed through the belly)

3. Blood transfusions or blood products

4. Artificial nutrition and hydration (given through a tube in a vein or in the stomach)

5. Simple diagnostic tests (for example, blood tests or x-rays), **or antibiotics** (drugs to fight infection)

6. Pain medications, even if they dull consciousness and indirectly shorten my life

THE GOAL OF MEDICAL CARE SHOULD BE (*check one*):

SITUATION A

If I am in a coma or a persistent vegetative state and, in the opinion of my physician and two consultants, have no known hope of regaining awareness and higher mental functions no matter what is done, then my wishes — if medically reasonable — for this and any additional illness would be:

I want	I want treatment tried. If no clear improvement, stop.	I am undecided	I do not want
	Not applicable		
	Not applicable		
	Not applicable		
	Not applicable		

___ prolong life; treat everything
___ choose quality of life over longevity
___ provide comfort care only
___ other (*please specify*):_____
_____

SITUATION B

If I am in a coma and, in the opinion of my physician and two consultants, have a small but uncertain chance of regaining higher mental functions, a somewhat greater chance of surviving with permanent brain damage, and a much greater chance of not recovering at all, then my wishes — if medically reasonable — for this and any additional illness would be:

I want	I want treatment tried. If no clear improvement, stop.	I am undecided	I do not want
	Not applicable		
	Not applicable		
	Not applicable		
	Not applicable		

___ prolong life; treat everything
___ attempt to cure, but reevaluate often
___ choose quality of life over longevity
___ provide comfort care only
___ other (*please specify*):_____
_____

SITUATION C

If I have brain damage or some brain disease that in the opinion of my physician and two consultants cannot be reversed and that makes me unable to recognize people, to speak meaningfully to them, or to live independently, *and I also have a terminal illness,* then my wishes — if medically reasonable — for this and any additional illness would be:

I want	I want treatment tried. If no clear improvement, stop.	I am undecided	I do not want
	Not applicable		
	Not applicable		
	Not applicable		
	Not applicable		

___ prolong life; treat everything
___ attempt to cure, but reevaluate often
___ choose quality of life over longevity
___ provide comfort care only
___ other (*please specify*):_____

SITUATION D

If I have brain damage or some brain disease that in the opinion of my physician and two consultants cannot be reversed and that makes me unable to recognize people, to speak meaningfully to them, or to live independently, *but I have no terminal illness,* then my wishes — if medically reasonable — for this and any additional illness would be:

I want	I want treatment tried. If no clear improvement, stop.	I am undecided	I do not want
	Not applicable		
	Not applicable		
	Not applicable		
	Not applicable		

___ prolong life; treat everything
___ attempt to cure, but reevaluate often
___ choose quality of life over longevity
___ provide comfort care only
___ other (*please specify*):_____

SITUATION E

If, in the opinion of my physician and two consultants, I have an incurable chronic illness that involves mental disability or physical suffering and ultimately causes death, and in addition I have an illness that is immediately life threatening but reversible, and I am temporarily unable to make decisions, then my wishes — if medically reasonable — would be:

I want	I want treatment tried. If no clear improvement, stop.	I am undecided	I do not want
	Not applicable		
	Not applicable		
	Not applicable		
	Not applicable		

___ prolong life; treat everything
___ attempt to cure, but reevaluate often
___ choose quality of life over longevity
___ provide comfort care only
___ other (*please specify*):_____

SITUATION F

If I am in my current state of health (*describe briefly*):_____

_____

and then have an illness that, in the opinion of my physician and two consultants, is life threatening but reversible, and I am temporarily unable to make decisions, then my wishes — if medically reasonable — would be:

I want	I want treatment tried. If no clear improvement, stop.	I am undecided	I do not want
	Not applicable		
	Not applicable		
	Not applicable		
	Not applicable		

___ prolong life; treat everything
___ attempt to cure, but reevaluate often
___ choose quality of life over longevity
___ provide comfort care only
___ other (*please specify*):_____

MY PERSONAL STATEMENT
(use another page if necessary)

Please mention anything that would be important for your physician and your proxy to know. In particular, try to answer the following questions: 1) What medical conditions, if any, would make living so unpleasant that you would want life-sustaining treatment *withheld*? (Intractable pain? Irreversible mental damage? Inability to share love? Dependence on others? Another condition you would regard as intolerable?) 2) Under what medical circumstances would you want to *stop* interventions that might already have been started?

Should there be any difference between my preferences detailed in the illness situations and those understood from my goals or from my personal statement, I wish my treatment selections / my goals / my personal statement (*please delete as appropriate*) to be given greater weight.

When I am dying, I would like — if my proxy and my health-care team think it is reasonable — to be cared for:

- ☐ at home or in a hospice
- ☐ in a nursing home
- ☐ in a hospital
- ☐ other (*please specify*): _____

ORGAN DONATION
(please check boxes and fill in blanks where appropriate)

__ I hereby make this anatomical gift, to take effect after my death:

I give
- ☐ my body
- ☐ any needed organs or parts
- ☐ the following parts: _____

to
- ☐ the following person or institution: _____
- ☐ the physician in attendance at my death
- ☐ the hospital in which I die
- ☐ the following physician, hospital storage bank, or other medical institution: _____

for
- ☐ any purpose authorized by law
- ☐ therapy of another person
- ☐ medical education
- ☐ transplantation
- ☐ research

__ I do not wish to make any anatomical gift from my body.

DURABLE POWER OF ATTORNEY FOR HEALTH CARE

I appoint as my proxy decision-maker(s):

_____
Name and Address

and (*optional*)

_____
Name and Address

I direct my proxy to make health-care decisions based on his/her assessment of my personal wishes. If my personal desires are unknown, my proxy is to make health-care decisions based on his/her best guess as to my wishes. My proxy shall have the authority to make all health-care decisions for me, including decisions about life-sustaining treatment, if I am unable to make them myself. My proxy's authority becomes effective if my attending physician determines in writing that I lack the capacity to make or to communicate health-care decisions. My proxy is then to have the same authority to make health-care decisions as I would if I had the capacity to make them, EXCEPT (*list the limitations, if any, you wish to place on your proxy's authority*):

Should there be any disagreement between the wishes I have indicated in this document and the decisions favored by my above-named proxy, I wish my proxy to have authority over my written statements / I wish my written statements to bind my proxy. (*Please delete as necessary.*) If I have appointed more than one proxy and there is disagreement between their wishes, _____ _____ shall have final authority.

Signed: _____
        Signature   Printed Name

        _____
        Address   Date

Witness: _____
        Signature   Printed Name

        _____
        Address   Date

Witness: _____
        Signature   Printed Name

        _____
        Address   Date

Physician (*optional*):

I am _____'s physician. I have seen this advance care document and have had an opportunity to discuss his/her preferences regarding medical interventions at the end of life. If _____ becomes incompetent, I understand that it is my duty to interpret and implement the preferences contained in this document in order to fulfill his/her wishes.

        _____
        Signature   Printed Name

        _____
        Address   Date

Revised 8/91

This form was original published as part of an article by Linda L. Emanuel and Ezekiel J. Emanuel, "The Medical Directive: A New Comprehensive Advance Care Document" in *Journal of the American Medical Association* June 9, 1989;261:3290. It does not reflect the official policy of the American Medical Association.

Copies of this form may be obtained from the Harvard Medical School Health Publications Group, P.O. Box 380, Boston, MA 02117 at 2 copies for $5 or 5 copies for $10; bulk orders also available.

APPENDIX D

A Patient's Bill of Rights

Introduction

Effective health care requires collaboration between patients and physicians and other health care professionals. Open and honest communication, respect for personal and professional values, and sensitivity to differences are integral to optimal patient care. As the setting for the provision of health services, hospitals must provide a foundation for understanding and respecting the rights and responsibilities of patients, their families, physicians, and other caregivers. Hospitals must ensure a health care ethic that respects the role of patients in decision making about treatment choices and other aspects of their care. Hospitals must be sensitive to cultural, racial, linguistic, religious, age, gender, and other differences as well as the needs of persons with disabilities.

The American Hospital Association presents *A Patient's Bill of Rights* with the expectation that it will contribute to more effective patient care and be supported by the hospital on behalf of the institution, its medical staff, employees, and patients. The American Hospital Association encourages health care institutions to tailor this bill of rights to their patient community by translating and/or simplifying the language of this bill of rights as may be necessary to ensure that patients and their families understand their rights and responsibilities.

Bill of Rights*

1. The patient has the right to considerate and respectful care.

2. The patient has the right to and is encouraged to obtain from physicians and other direct caregivers relevant, current, and understandable information concerning diagnosis, treatment, and prognosis.

   Except in emergencies when the patient lacks decision-making capacity and the need for treatment is urgent, the patient is entitled to the opportunity to discuss and request information related to the specific procedures and/or treatments, the risks involved, the possible length of recuperation, and the medically reasonable alternatives and their accompanying risks and benefits.

   Patients have the right to know the identity of physicians, nurses, and others involved in their care, as well as when those involved are students, residents, or other trainees. The patient also has the right to know the immediate and long-term financial implications of treatment choices, insofar as they are known.

3. The patient has the right to make decisions about the plan of care prior to and during the course of treatment and to refuse a recommended treatment or plan of care to the extent permitted by law and hospital policy and to be informed of the medical consequences of this action. In case of

such refusal, the patient is entitled to other appropriate care and services that the hospital provides or transfer to another hospital. The hospital should notify patients of any policy that might affect patient choice within the institution.

4. The patient has the right to have an advance directive (such as a living will, health care proxy, or durable power of attorney for health care) concerning treatment or designating a surrogate decision maker with the expectation that the hospital will honor the intent of that directive to the extent permitted by law and hospital policy.

   Health care institutions must advise patients of their rights under state law and hospital policy to make informed medical choices, ask if the patient has an advance directive, and include that information in patient records. The patient has the right to timely information about hospital policy that may limit its ability to implement fully a legally valid advance directive.

5. The patient has the right to every consideration of privacy. Case discussion, consultation, examination, and treatment should be conducted so as to protect each patient's privacy.

These rights can be exercised on the patient's behalf by a designated surrogate or proxy decision maker if the patient lacks decision-making capacity, is legally incompetent, or is a minor.

A Patient's Bill of Rights was first adopted by the American Hospital Association in 1973. This revision was approved by the AHA Board of Trustees on October 21, 1992.

6. The patient has the right to expect that all communications and records pertaining to his/her care will be treated as confidential by the hospital, except in cases such as suspected abuse and public health hazards when reporting is permitted or required by law. The patient has the right to expect that the hospital will emphasize the confidentiality of this information when it releases it to any other parties entitled to review information in these records.

7. The patient has the right to review the records pertaining to his/her medical care and to have the information explained or interpreted as necessary, except when restricted by law.

8. The patient has the right to expect that, within its capacity and policies, a hospital will make reasonable response to the request of a patient for appropriate and medically indicated care and services. The hospital must provide evaluation, service, and/or referral as indicated by the urgency of the case. When medically appropriate and legally permissible, or when a patient has so requested, a patient may be transferred to another facility. The institution to which the patient is to be transferred must first have accepted the patient for transfer. The patient must also have the benefit of complete information and explanation concerning the need for, risks, benefits, and alternatives to such a transfer.

9. The patient has the right to ask and be informed of the existence of business relationships among the hospital, educational institutions, other health care providers, or payers that may influence the patient's treatment and care.

10. The patient has the right to consent to or decline to participate in proposed research studies or human experimentation affecting care and treatment or requiring direct patient involvement, and to have those studies fully explained prior to consent. A patient who declines to participate in research or experimentation is entitled to the most effective care that the hospital can otherwise provide.

11. The patient has the right to expect reasonable continuity of care when appropriate and to be informed by physicians and other caregivers of available and realistic patient care options when hospital care is no longer appropriate.

12. The patient has the right to be informed of hospital policies and practices that relate to patient care, treatment, and responsibilities. The patient has the right to be informed of available resources for resolving disputes, grievances, and conflicts, such as ethics committees, patient representatives, or other mechanisms available in the institution. The patient has the right to be informed of the hospital's charges for services and available payment methods.

The collaborative nature of health care requires that patients, or their families/surrogates, participate in their care. The effectiveness of care and patient satisfaction with the course of treatment depend, in part, on the patient fulfilling certain responsibilities. Patients are responsible for providing information about past illnesses, hospitalizations, medications, and other matters related to health status. To participate effectively in decision making, patients must be encouraged to take responsibility for requesting additional information or clarification about their health status or treatment when they do not fully understand information and instructions. Patients are also responsible for ensuring that the health care institution has a copy of their written advance directive if they have one. Patients are responsible for informing their physicians and other caregivers if they anticipate problems in following prescribed treatment.

Patients should also be aware of the hospital's obligation to be reasonably efficient and equitable in providing care to other patients and the community. The hospital's rules and regulations are designed to help the hospital meet this obligation. Patients and their families are responsible for making reasonable accommodations to the needs of the hospital, other patients, medical staff, and hospital employees. Patients are responsible for providing necessary information for insurance claims and for working with the hospital to make payment arrangements, when necessary.

A person's health depends on much more than health care services. Patients are responsible for recognizing the impact of their life-style on their personal health.

Conclusion

Hospitals have many functions to perform, including the enhancement of health status, health promotion, and the prevention and treatment of injury and disease; the immediate and ongoing care and rehabilitation of patients; the education of health professionals, patients, and the community; and research. All these activities must be conducted with an overriding concern for the values and dignity of patients.

Reprinted with permission from the *AHA Guide to the Health Care Field,* copyright 1992 by the American Hospital Association.

Your Rights As a Hospital Patient

We consider you a partner in your hospital care. When you are well-informed, participate in treatment decisions, and communicate openly with your doctor and other health professionals, you help make your care as effective as possible. This hospital encourages respect for the personal preferences and values of each individual.

While you are a patient in the hospital, your rights include the following:

1. You have the right to considerate and respectful care.

2. You have the right to be well-informed about your illness, possible treatments, and likely outcome and to discuss this information with your doctor. You have the right to know the names and roles of people treating you.

3. You have the right to consent to or refuse a treatment, as permitted by law, throughout your hospital stay. If you refuse a recommended treatment, you will receive other needed and available care.

4. You have the right to have an advance directive, such as a living will or health care proxy. These documents express your choices about your future care or name someone to decide if you cannot speak for yourself. If you have a written advance directive, you should provide a copy to the hospital, your family, and your doctor.

5. You have the right to privacy. The hospital, your doctor, and others caring for you will protect your privacy as much as possible.

6. You have the right to expect that treatment records are confidential unless you have given permission to give out information or reporting is required or permitted by law. When the hospital releases records to others, such as insurers, it emphasized that the records are confidential.

7. You have the right to review your medical records and to have the information explained, except when restricted by law.

8. You have the right to expect that the hospital will give you necessary health services to the best of its ability. Treatment, referral, or transfer may be recommended. If transfer is recommended or requested, you will be informed of risks, benefits, and alternatives. You will not be transferred until the other institution agrees to accept you.

9. You have the right to know if this hospital has relationships with outside parties that may influence your treatment and care. These relationships may be with educational institutions, other health care providers, or insurers.

10. You have the right to consent or decline to take part in research affecting your care. If you choose not to take part, you will receive the most effective care the hospital otherwise provides.

11. You have the right to be told of realistic care alternatives when hospital care is no longer appropriate.

12. You have the right to know about hospital rules that affect you and your treatment and about charges and payment methods. You have the right to know about hospital resources, such as patient representatives or ethics committees, that can help you resolve problems and questions about your hospital stay and care.

You have responsibilities as a patient. You are responsible for providing information about your health, including past illnesses, hospital stays, and use of medicine. You are responsible for asking questions when you do not understand information or instructions. If you believe you can't follow through with your treatment, you are responsible for telling your doctor.

This hospital works to provide care efficiently and fairly to all patients and the community. You and your visitors are responsible for being considerate of the needs of other patients, staff, and the hospital. You are responsible for providing information for insurance and for working with the hospital to arrange payment, when needed.

Your health depends not just on your hospital care but, in the long term, on the decisions you make in your daily life. You are responsible for recognizing the effect of lifestyle on your personal health.

A hospital serves many purposes. Hospitals work to improve people's health, treat people with injury and disease; educate doctors, health professionals, patients, and community members; and improve understanding of health and disease. In carrying out these activities, this institution works to respect your values and dignity.

APPENDIX E

ADVANCE DIRECTIVE
Living Will and Health Care Proxy

D *eath is a part of life. It is a reality like birth, growth and aging. I am using this advance directive to convey my wishes about medical care to my doctors and other people looking after me at the end of my life. It is called an advance directive because it gives instructions in advance about what I want to happen to me in the future. It expresses my wishes about medical treatment that might keep me alive. I want this to be legally binding.*

If I cannot make or communicate decisions about my medical care, those around me should rely on this document for instructions about measures that could keep me alive.

I do not want medical treatment (including feeding and water by tube) that will keep me alive if:
- I am unconscious and there is no reasonable prospect that I will ever be conscious again (even if I am not going to die soon in my medical condition), or
- I am near death from an illness or injury with no reasonable prospect of recovery.

I do want medicine and other care to make me more comfortable and to take care of pain and suffering. I want this even if the pain medicine makes me die sooner.

I want to give some extra instructions: [*Here list any special instructions, e.g., some people fear being kept alive after a debilitating stroke. If you have wishes about this, or any other conditions, please write them here.*]

**The legal language in the box that follows is a health care proxy.
It gives another person the power to make medical decisions for me.**

I name _____, who lives at _____

_____, phone number _____.

to make medical decisions for me if I cannot make them myself. This person is called a health care "surrogate," "agent," "proxy," or "attorney in fact." This power of attorney shall become effective when I become incapable of making or communicating decisions about my medical care. This means that this document stays legal when and if I lose the power to speak for myself, for instance, if I am in a coma or have Alzheimer's disease.

My health care proxy has power to tell others what my advance directive means. This person also has power to make decisions for me, based either on what I would have wanted, or, if this is not known, on what he or she thinks is best for me.

If my first choice health care proxy cannot or decides not to act for me, I name _____

_____, address _____,

phone number _____, as my second choice.

(continued on other side)

I have discussed my wishes with my health care proxy, and with my second choice if I have chosen to appoint a second person. My proxy(ies) has(have) agreed to act for me.

I have thought about this advance directive carefully. I know what it means and want to sign it. I have chosen two witnesses, neither of whom is a member of my family, nor will inherit from me when I die. My witnesses are not the same people as those I named as my health care proxies. I understand that this form should be notarized if I use the box to name (a) health care proxy(ies).

Signature _____

Date _____

Address _____

Witness' signature _____

Witness' printed name _____

Address _____

Witness' signature _____

Witness' printed name _____

Address _____

Notary [to be used if proxy is appointed] _____

Drafted and distributed by Choice In Dying, Inc.—the national council for the right to die. Choice In Dying is a national not-for-profit organization which works for the rights of patients at the end of life. In addition to this generic advance directive, Choice In Dying distributes advance directives that conform to each state's specific legal requirements and maintains a national Living Will Registry for completed documents.

CHOICE IN DYING, INC.—
the national council for the right to die
(formerly Concern for Dying/Society for the Right to Die)
200 Varick Street, New York, NY 10014   (212) 366-5540

Reprinted by permission.

APPENDIX F

EXAMPLE OF A
DURABLE POWER OF ATTORNEY

**STATE OF TEXAS DURABLE POWER OF ATTORNEY
FOR HEALTH CARE**

(Note: The Texas Durable Power of Attorney for Health Care is included as an example because of its thorough disclosure form. This disclosure summarizes considerations such as the importance of knowing the requirements of your state's DPAHC law, the power that a health care agent (attorney-in-fact) is given through a DPAHC or DPA, and the importance of stating your wishes regarding medical treatment [in writing] and discussing them with your agent and your doctor. If your state does not have a DPAHC law, these instructions are applicable, nevertheless, and you can use the form as a guide for preparing you own DPAHC appointment.)

DISCLOSURE STATEMENT:
Information Concerning the Durable Power of Attorney for Health Care: This is an important legal document. Before signing the document you should know these important facts:

Except to the extent you state otherwise, this document gives the person you name as your agent the authority to make any and all health care decisions for you in accordance with your wishes, including your religious and moral beliefs, when you are no longer capable of making them yourself. Because "Health Care" means any treatment, service, or procedure to maintain, diagnose, or treat your physical or mental condition, your agent has the power to make a broad range of health care decisions for you. Your agent may consent, refuse to consent, or withdraw consent to medical treatment and may make decisions about withdrawing or withholding life-sustaining treatment. Your agent may not consent to voluntary inpatient mental health services, convulsive treatment, psychotherapy, or abortion. (Note: Most state DPAHC laws do not contain such specific restrictions.) A physician must comply with your agent's instructions or allow you to be transferred to another physician.

Your agent's authority begins when your doctor certifies that you lack the capacity to make health care decisions.

Your agent is obligated to follow your instructions when making decisions on your behalf. Unless you state otherwise, your agent has the same authority to make decisions about your health care as you would have had.

It is important that you discuss this document with your physician or other health care provider before you sign it to make sure that you understand the nature and range of decisions that may be made on your behalf. If you do not have a physician, you should talk with someone else who is knowledgeable about these issues and can answer your questions. You do not need a lawyer's assistance to complete this document, but if there is anything in this document that you do not understand, you should ask a lawyer to explain it to you.

The person you appoint to be your health care agent should be someone you know and trust. The person must be 18 years of age or older or a person under 18 years who has had the disabilities of minority removed. (Note: This provision is unique to the Texas law. Most states do not address the issue of a minor as an agent.) If you appoint your health or residential care provider, e.g., your physician or an employee of a home health agency, hospital, nursing home, or residential care home, other than a relative, that person has to choose between acting as your agent and acting as your health or residential care provider; the law does not permit a person to do both at the same time. (Note: Many state DPAHC laws do not contain these restrictions on who can serve as agent.)

You should inform the person you appoint that you want the person to be your health care agent. You should discuss this document with your agent and your physician and give each a signed copy. You should indicate on the document itself the people and institutions who have signed copies. Your agent is not liable for health care decisions made in good faith on your behalf.

Even after you have signed this document, you have the right to make health care decisions for yourself as long as you are able to do so, and treatment cannot be given to you or stopped over your objection. You have the right to revoke the authority granted to your agent by informing your agent or your health or residential care provider orally or in writing, or by your execution of a subsequent durable power of attorney for health care. Unless you state otherwise, your appointment of a spouse dissolves on divorce.

This document may not be changed or modified. If you want to make changes in the document, you must make an entirely new one.

You may wish to designate an alternate agent in the event that your agent is unwilling, unable, or ineligible to act as your agent. Any alternate agent you designate has the same authority to make health care decisions for you.

This power of attorney is not valid unless it is signed in the presence of two or more qualified witnesses. The following persons may not act as witnesses:

1. The person you have designated as your agent.
2. Your health or residential care provider or an employee of your health or residential care provider.
3. Your spouse.
4. Your lawful heirs or beneficiaries named in your will or a deed.
5. Creditors or persons who have a claim against you.

DURABLE POWER OF ATTORNEY FOR HEALTH CARE

DESIGNATION OF HEALTH CARE AGENT:
I, _____ (insert your name), appoint:
Name: _____
Address: _____
_____ Phone _____

as my agent to make any and all health care decisions for me, except to the extent that I state otherwise in this document. This durable power of attorney for health care takes effect if I become unable to make my own health care decisions and this fact is certified in writing by my physician.

LIMITATIONS ON THE DECISION MAKING AUTHORITY OF MY AGENT ARE AS FOLLOWS: _____
_____
_____
_____

DESIGNATION OF ALTERNATE AGENT:
(You are not required to designate an alternate agent but you may do so. An alternate agent may make the same health care decisions as the designated agent if the designated agent is unable or unwilling to act as your agent. If the designated agent is your spouse, the designation is automatically revoked by law if your marriage is dissolved.)

   If the person designated as my agent is unable or unwilling to make health care decisions for me, I designate the following persons to serve as my agent to make health care decisions for me as authorized by this document and to serve in the following order:

   A. First Alternate Agent:
Name: _____
Address: _____
_____ Phone _____

   B. Second Alternate Agent:
Name_____
Address: _____
_____ Phone _____

The original of this document is kept at: _____
The following individuals or institutions have signed copies:
Names and addresses:

_____
_____

DURATION:
I understand that this power of attorney exists indefinitely from the date I execute this document unless I establish a shorter time or revoke the power of attorney. If I am unable to make health care decisions for myself when this power of attorney expires, the authority I have granted my agent continues to exist until the time I become able to make health care decisions for myself.
(IF APPLICABLE) This power of attorney ends on the following date:

_____

PRIOR DESIGNATIONS REVOKED:
I revoke any prior power of attorney for health care.

ACKNOWLEDGMENT OF DISCLOSURE STATEMENT:
I have been provided with a disclosure statement explaining the effect of this document. I have read and understood the information contained in the disclosure statement.

YOU MUST DATE AND SIGN THIS POWER OF ATTORNEY. (Note: Sign in the presence of the witnesses.)

I sign my name to this durable power of attorney for health care on
_____day of _____19___ at: (City and State)_____
Signature: _____
Print Name:_____

STATEMENT OF WITNESSES:
I declare under penalty of perjury that the principal has identified himself or herself to me, that the principal signed or acknowledged this durable power of attorney in my presence, that I believe the principal to be of sound mind, that the principal has affirmed that he or she is aware of the nature of the document and is signing it voluntarily and free from duress, that the principal requested that I serve as witness to his or her execution of this document, that I am not the person appointed as agent by this document, and that I am not a provider of health or residential care, an employee of a provider of health or residential care, the operator of a community care facility, or an employee of an operator of a health care facility.

I declare that I am not related to the principal by blood, marriage, or adoption and that to the best of my knowledge, I am not entitled to any part of the estate of the principal on the death of the principal under a will or by operation of law.

Witness signature:_____
Print Name:_____
Address: _____
Witness Signature: _____
Print Name:_____Date _____
Address: _____

Source: Tex. Civ. Prac. & Rem. Code Ann. 135.015–.016 (Vernon Supp. 1992)

APPENDIX G

BIBLIOGRAPHY

The following are some books and articles that I have found helpful in addition to those cited in the End Notes. Most are available in libraries and bookstores, but you might have to ask your librarian for assistance in securing some of the journal articles.

ADVANCE DIRECTIVES FOR MEDICAL TREATMENT

Collins, Evan R., Jr., and Doron Weber. *The Complete Guide to Living Wills.* New York: Bantam Books, 1991. Contains advice on writing an advance directive and a guide to the various state laws related to advance directives plus copies of the forms for each state.

Emanuel, Linda, and Ezekiel Emanuel. *The Medical Directive.* Boston: Harvard Medical School Health Publications Group. A portion of this directive is included in Appendix C. Copies of the entire packet, which includes a durable power of attorney form, can be ordered from the Harvard Medical School Health Publications Group, P.O. Box 380, Boston, MA 02117. Two copies for $5, five copies for $10; bulk orders also available.

Outerbridge, David E., and Alan R. Hersch. *Easing the Passage.* New York: Harper Collins, 1991. One of the authors is a family physician, so although this book does not contain an extensive discussion of advance directives, the discussion of medical situations and procedures, case studies, patients' rights, hospice, and other issues adds depth to an understanding of terminal care decisions.

COURT DECISIONS

Cases that reach the appellate level can be found in law journals or the computerized directories (LEXUS). Trial court decisions are not as readily available. Choice in Dying prepares fact sheets summarizing right-to-die cases, which provide a citation number to use in searching for the entire decision. There is a charge for the fact sheets, which are updated annually. Choice in Dying, 200 Varick Street, New York, NY 10014, 212/366-5540.

EUTHANASIA

Bender, David L., and Neal Bernards, eds. *Euthanasia, Opposing Viewpoints.* Detroit: Greenhaven Press, 1989. Part of the Opposing Viewpoints series, this book presents opposing views on such questions as "Is euthanasia ethical?" "What policy should guide euthanasia?" "What criteria should influence euthanasia decisions?" "Is infant euthanasia ethical?" "Who should make the euthanasia decision?" (This chapter contains opposing viewpoints on living wills, again perpetuating the misunderstanding about living wills and euthanasia!)

Hamel, Ron. *Choosing Death: Active Euthanasia, Religion, and the Public Debate.* Philadelphia: Trinity Press, 1991. This book, a publication of the Park Ridge Center for the Study of Health, Faith, and Ethics, contains a historical view of euthanasia, views of the major religious faiths and traditions, and differing viewpoints of bioethicists, nurses, physicians, and religious scholars about the justification for euthanasia and whether there should be public policy on euthanasia.

Humphrey, Derek. *Dying with Dignity.* New York: Birth Lane Press, 1992. Humphrey, who wrote *Final Exit*, differentiates between mercy killing, which he calls the *unrequested* taking of another's life, and helping another person to commit suicide. He describes the major mercy killing cases in this country and gives reasons for his belief that voluntary euthansia will become lawful in the United States within the next few years. He does *not* confuse euthanasia with withholding or withdrawing life-sustaining treatment.

FINANCIAL CONSIDERATIONS

Esperti, Robert A., and Renno L. Peterson. *Loving Trust: The Right Way to Provide for Yourself and Guarantee the Future of Your Loved Ones.* New York: Viking Press, 1988. The authors are strong advocates of trusts, and their reasons are persuasive, so readers should place the information in perspective. This book provides thought-provoking examples and questions to think about as you consider a financial directive.

Hughes, Theodore E., and David Klein. *A Family Guide to Wills, Funerals, and Probate: How to Protect Yourself and Your Survivors.* New York: Charles Scribner's Sons, 1987. This is an overview of issues related to financial directives and considerations such as planning a funeral. The characteristics, advantages, and disadvantages of the various types of wills and trusts are discussed, as are probate and how to avoid it; estate taxes and how to pay no more than your fair share; and the duties of the personal representative. Readers should find the extensive discussion of funeral arrangements and alternatives helpful. The chapter on living wills, because it is based on the laws and practices of the early 1980's, is incomplete, however. Nevertheless, it contains useful information for people beginning the process of preparing a financial directive.

Roberson, Cliff. *Avoiding Probate: Tamper-Proof Estate Planning.* Blue Ridge Summit, PA: Liberty House, 1989. This book contains relatively recent information about financial directives: the basics of estate planning; a description of various types of wills and trusts, their advantages and disadvantages. It discusses life insurance and real estate considerations and probate issues. (I was amused to find that in my copy, which I got at a local library, the chapter entitled "Drafting a Will That Will Stand Up in Court" was highlighted by a previous reader!) The discussion of living wills is limited, but the remainder of the information, including sample IRS forms and a glossary of legal terms, is clearly written and useful.

HEALTH INSURANCE AND MEDICARE

National Association of Insurance Commissioners and the Health Care Financing Administration of the U.S. Department of Health and Human Services. *Guide to Health Insurance for People with Medicare.* Washington, D.C.: U.S. Government Printing Office. This publication describes Medicare benefits, deductibles, and copayments in effect in 1992 and provides advice on evaluating supplemental (Medigap) policies. It is for sale by the U.S. Government Printing Office, Superintendent of Documents, Mail Stop SSOP, Washington, DC 20402-9328.

The Social Security Administration also has publications on Medicare and other issues related to retirement. Check with your local social security office or library.

HOSPICE

Stoddard, Sandal. *The Hospice Movement.* Briarcliff Manor, NY: Stein and Day, 1978. This book was written for laypeople by a volunteer in St. Christopher's Hospital Hospice in London, a pioneer among modern hospice programs. Although this book was written more than 15 years ago, the information and insights are timely.

Zimmerman, Jack McKay. *Hospice: Complete Care for the Terminally Ill.* Baltimore: Urban and Schwarzenberg, 1986. The author, a physician, established the hospice program at Church Hospital, Baltimore, Md. Various members of the hospice program contribute chapters, so the perspective is broad. This is an extensive discussion of the many aspects of hospice care, including general aspects of hospice care and its philosophy; medical issues such as relief of physical symptoms and the role for hospice care in medicine; hospice for terminal illnesses other than cancer; psycho-social, spiritual, and bioethical issues related to hospice; administration of hospice programs; the role of volunteers and of inpatient and outpatient hospice care; bereavement care; and the future of hospice. It is a useful book for both consumers and providers of health care.

LIVING AND DYING

Bender, David, and Bruno Leone, eds. *Death and Dying: Opposing Viewpoints.* St. Paul, MN: Greenhaven Press, 1987. Presents opposite viewpoints on how to cope with death, how suicide can be prevented, infant euthanasia, and alternative care for dying people. The different perspectives are thought-provoking.

Beisser, Arnold R. *A Graceful Passage: Notes on the Freedom to Live or Die.* New York: Bantam Books, 1991. The author is a physician who at age 25 contracted polio and became permanently paralyzed; only the muscles in his face, part of his neck, and part of his right hand retained function. He has been on a respirator for the past 40 years. In spite of his paralysis, he has been able to practice medicine, teach, and write. His experiences and insights challenge us to examine our feelings and beliefs about life and death.

Homer, Paul, and Martha Holstein, eds. *A Good Old Age: The Paradox of Setting Limits.* New York: Touchstone Books, 1990. Contains foreword and afterword sections by Daniel Callahan plus a collection of writings by medical ethicists, economists, gerontologists, theologians, and public policy analysts and commentators. Addresses the topic of allocating health care resources and setting limits on the cost of health care from multiple perspectives.

Kubler-Ross, Elisabeth and Mal Warshaw (photographer). *To Live until We Say Goodbye.* Englewood Cliffs, N.J.: Prentice-Hall, 1978. Stories and photos of individuals facing death (including one about the puzzlement and hurt that one daughter felt because of the terms of her mother's will. Kubler-Ross is a psychiatrist, world-renowned for her writings on death and dying, including *On Death and Dying*, published in 1969, in which she set forth the idea of five stages of dying. Although these stages have been criticized by others, she made a major contribution by being the first to talk and write about death, thus breaking a taboo in medicine and the popular media.

Shannon, Thomas A., and Charles N. Faso. *Let Them Go Free: Family Prayer Service to Assist in the Withdrawal of Life Support Systems.* Kansas City, Mo.:

Sheed and Ward. Available from the publisher at 115 East Armour Boulevard, Kansas City, MO 64141.

THE PATIENT SELF-DETERMINATION ACT

Advance Directives Protocols and the PSDA. Information for health care professionals regarding policies and guidelines for handling advance directives. Contains sample protocols, a copy of the PSDA, and a summary of the law's requirements. Available for $10 from Choice in Dying, 200 Varick Street, 10th Floor, New York, NY 10014, 212/366-5540.

Interim Final Rule. CFR parts 417, et al. Federal Register, March 6, 1992. pp. 8194-8204.

The Patient Self-Determination Directory and Resource Guide. A directory of national and local organizations that can provide education and technical assistance on advance directives. National Health Lawyers Association, Development Office, 1820 Eye Street NW, Suite 900, Washington, DC 20036.

STATEMENTS OF RELIGIOUS GROUPS

Connelly, R.J. "Natural Death and Christian Fasting." *Journal of Religion and Health* 25, no. 3, Fall 1986. This article addresses tube feeding from a religious perspective. It upholds the undue burden principle in making decisions as to the morality of providing or withholding medical treatment.

Declaration on Euthanasia, the Sacred Congregation for the Doctrine of Faith, Vatican City, May 5, 1980. This statement affirms the reverence for live and "the lofty dignity of the human person, and in a special way his or her right to life." It is a reminder of statements made by past Popes, including Pope Pius XII's ordinary versus extraordinary measures and the principle of double effect but acknowledges the need to examine the effect of progress in medical science on dying. The principle of "Due Proportion in the Use of Remedies" is set forth, meaning that the proportionality of benefit and burden to patient and family should be considered when determining if it is right to provide medical treatment to a dying person. The Declaration is included in the appendix to *Forgoing Life-Sustaining Treatment,* which was published in 1983 by the President's Commission on Ethical Issues in Medicine and Biomedical and Behavioral Research. This book provides an excellent overview of ethical issues related to medical treatment at the end of life, but it is out of print; you might be able to find a copy in a library. You might be able to get a copy of the Vatican Declaration from a parish priest or the office of an Archdiocese. If not, contact the Catholic Health Association, 4455 Woodson Road, St. Louis, MO 63134.

Melton, Gordon, and Christel Manning, eds. *The Churches Speak: On Euthanasia.* Detroit: Gale Research, 1991. Contains formal statements and position papers on the topic of euthanasia from most of the major religions in the world. Although most of the statements include "euthanasia" in their titles, a distinction is made between the deliberate taking of life, even though the intent is to achieve a good death, and withholding or withdrawing life-sustaining treatment. Most use futility and burdensomeness as criteria in decisions to forgo treatment.

APPENDIX H

RESOURCES

Choice in Dying, Inc. (formerly Concern for Dying and the Society for the Right to Die), 200 Varick Street, 10th Floor, New York, NY 10014, 212/366-5540. This unique organization provides many services related to advance directives and patients' rights to refuse life-sustaining treatment. These services include the following:

- Information about advance directives, the laws of each state, and copies of the forms to use.
- A confidential registry of advance directives. This service includes a review of the directive to see that it is properly executed, a wallet card with the personal registry number, and 24-hour telephone service. The charge is $35 for members, $40 for nonmembers.
- Legal services and advocacy for people and families whose wishes or directives are not being honored.
- Educational material, including publications and videos on a variety of subjects such as advance directives, summaries of major right-to-die court cases, and the Patient Self-Determination Act.

Minimum membership contribution is $15, which includes a quarterly newsletter and discounts on publications.

STATE HOSPITAL ASSOCIATIONS

Alabama Hospital Association
500 North East Boulevard
P.O. Box 17059
Montgomery, AL 36117
205/272-8781

Alaska State Hospital and Nursing Home Association
319 Seward Street, Suite 11
Juneau, AK 99801
907/586-1790

Arizona Hospital Association
1501 West Fountainhead Parkway
Suite 650
Tempe, AZ 85282
602/968-1083

Arkansas Hospital Association
419 Natural Resources Drive
Little Rock, AR 72205
501/224-7878

California Association of Hospitals and Health Systems
1201 K Street, Suite 800
P.O. Box 1100
Sacramento, CA 95812
916/443-7401

Colorado Hospital Association
2140 South Holly Street
Denver, CO 80222
303/758-1630

Association of Delaware Hospitals
1280 Governors Avenue
P.O. Box 471
Dover, DE 19901
302/674-2853

District of Columbia Hospital Association
1250 Eye Street NW, Suite 700
Washington, DC 20005
202/682-1581

Florida Hospital Association
307 Park Lake Circle
P.O. Box 531107
Orlando, FL 32853
407/841-6230

Georgia Hospital Association
North by Northwest Office Park
Atlanta, GA 30339
404/955-0324

Healthcare Association of Hawaii
932 Ward Avenue, Suite 430
Honolulu, HI 96814
808/521-8961

Idaho Hospital Association
Historic Hoff Building
802 West Bannock Street, Suite 500
Boise, ID 83702
208/338-5100

Illinois Hospital Association
Center for Health Affairs
1151 East Warrenville Road
P.O. Box 3015
Naperville, IL 60566
708/505-7777

Connecticut Hospital Association
110 Barnes Road
P.O. Box 90
Wallingford, CT 06492
203/265-7611

Indiana Hospital Association
One American Square
P.O. Box 82063
Indianapolis, IN 46282
317/633-4870

Iowa Hospital Association
100 East Grand Avenue, Suite 100
Des Moines, IA 50309
515/288-1955

Kansas Hospital Association
1263 Topeka Avenue
P.O. Box 2308
Topeka, KA 66601
913/233-7436

Kentucky Hospital Association
1302 Clear Spring Trace
P.O. Box 24163
Louisville, KY 40224
502/426-6220

Louisiana Hospital Association
9521 Brookline Avenue
P.O. Box 80720
Baton Rouge, LA 70898
504/928-0026

Maine Hospital Association
160 Capitol Street
Augusta, ME 04330
207/622-4794

Maryland Hospital Association
1301 York Road, Suite 800
Lutherville, MD 21093
301/321-6200

Massachusetts Hospital Association
5 New England Executive Park
Burlington, MA 01803
617/272-8000

Michigan Hospital Association
6215 West St. Joseph Highway
Lansing, MI 48917
517/323-3443

Minnesota Hospital Association
University Office Plaza, Suite 425
2221 University Avenue, SE
Minneapolis, MN 55414
612/331-5571

Mississippi Hospital Association
6425 Lakeover Road
P.O. Box 16444
Jackson, MS 39236
601/366-3962

Missouri Hospital Association
4713 Country Club Drive
P.O. Box 60
Jefferson City, MO 65102
314/893-3700

Montana Hospital Association
1720 Ninth Avenue
P.O. Box 5119
Helena, MT 59604
406/442-1911

Nebraska Hospital Association
1640 L Street, Suite D
Lincoln, NE 68508
402/476-0141

Nevada Hospital Association
4600 Kietzke Lane, Suite A-108
Reno, NV 89502
702/827-0184

New Hampshire Hospital Association
125 Airport Road
Concord, NH 03301
603/225-0900

New Jersey Hosp]ital Association
Center for Health Affairs
746-760 Alexander Road, CN 1
Princeton, NJ 08543
609/275-4000

New Mexico Hospital Association
2625 Pennsylvania Avenue, NE
Suite 2000, P.O. Box 36090
Albuquerque, NM 87176
505/889-3393

Hospital Association of New York State
74 Pearl Street
Albany, NY 12207
518/434-7600

North Carolina Hospital Association
2400 Weston Parkway
P.O. Box 80428
Raleigh, NC 27623
919/677-2400

North Dakota Hospital Association
Kirkwood Office Tower
919 South 7th Street
Bismarck, ND 58504
701//224-9732

Ohio Hospital Association
155 East Broad Street
Columbus, OH 43215
614/221-7614

Oklahoma Hospital Association
4000 Lincoln Boulevard
Oklahoma City, OK 73105
405/427-9537

Oregon Association of Hospitals
4000 Kruse Way Place
Building 2, Suite 100
Lake Oswego, OR 97035
503/636-2204

Hospital Association of Pennsylvania
4750 Lindle Road, P.O. Box 8600
Harrisburg, PA 17105
717/564-9200

Hospital Association of Rhode Island
Weld Building, 2nd Floor
345 Blackstone Boulevard
P.O. Box 9627
Providence, RI 02940
401/421-7100

South Carolina Hospital Association
101 Medical Circle
P.O. Box 6009
West Columbia, SC 29171
803/796-3080

South Dakota Hospital Association
3708 Brooks Place, Suite 1
Sioux Falls, SD 57106
605/361-2281

Tennessee Hospital Association
500 Interstate Boulevard South
Nashville, TN 37210
615/256-8240

Texas Hospital Association
6225 U.S.Highway 290 East
P.O. Box 15587
Austin, TX 78761
512/465-1000

Utah Hospital Association
515 South 700 East
Suite 2-D
Salt Lake City, UT 84102
801/364-1515

Vermont Hospital Association
148 Main Street
Montpelier, VT 05602
802/223-3461

Virginia Hospital Association
4200 Innslake Drive,
P.O. Box 31394
Richmond, VA 23294
804/747-8600

Washington State Hospital Association
190 Queen Avenue N
Seattle, WA 98109
206/281-7211

West Virginia Hospital Association
600 D Street
Second Level
South Charleston, WV 25303
304/744-9842

Wisconsin Hospital Association
5721 Odana Road
Madison, WI 53719
608/274-1820

Wyoming Hospital Association
2005 Warron Avenue
P.O. Box 5539
Cheyenne, WY 82003
307/632-9344

Source: Compiled from the *AHA Guide to the Health Care Field.* Chicago: American Hospital Association, 1991.

STATE BAR ASSOCIATIONS

Alabama State Bar
P.O. Box 671
Montgomery, AL 36101
205/269-1515

Alaska Bar Association
P.O. Box 100279
Anchorage, AK 99510
907/272-7469

State Bar of Arizona
363 North 1st Avenue
Phoenix, AZ 85003
602/252-4804

Arkansas Bar Association
400 West Markham
Little Rock, AR 72201
501/375-4605

State Bar of California
555 Franklin Street
San Francisco, CA 94102
415/561-8200

Colorado Bar Association
1900 Grant Street, #950
Denver, CO 80203
303/860-1115

Connecticut Bar Association
101 Corporate Place
Rocky Hill, CT 06067
203/721-0025

Delaware State Bar Association
P.O. Box 1709
Wilmington, DE 19899
302/658-5278

District of Columbia Bar
1707 L Street NW, Sixth Floor
Washington, DC 20036
202-331-3883

Florida Bar
650 Appalachee Parkway
Tallahassee, FL 32399
904/561-5600

State Bar of Georgia
800 The Hurt Building
50 Hurt Plaza
Atlanta, GA 30303
404/527-8700

Hawaii State Bar Association
P.O. Box 26
Honolulu, HI 96810
808/537-1868

Idaho State Bar
P.O. Box 895
Boise, ID 83701
208/342-8958

Illinois State Bar Association
424 South Second Street
Springfield, IL 62701
217/525-1760

Indiana State Bar Association
230 East Ohio, Sixth Floor
Indianapolis, IN 46204
317/639-5465

Iowa State Bar Association
1101 Fleming Building
Des Moines, IA 50309
515/243-3179

Kansas Bar Association
P.O. Box 1037
Topeka, KS 66601
913/234-5696

Kentucky Bar Association
West Main at Kentucky River
Frankfort, KY 40601
502/564-3795

Louisiana State Bar Association
601 St. Charles Avenue
New Orleans, LA 70130
504/566-1600

Maine State Bar Association
P.O. Box 788
Augusta, ME 04332
207/622-7523

Maryland State Bar Association
520 West Fayette Street
Baltimore, MD 21201
410/685-7878

Massachusetts Bar Association
20 West Street
Boston, MA 02111
617/542-3602

State Bar of Michigan
306 Townsend Street
Lansing, MI 48933
517/372-9030

Minnesota State Bar Association
430 Marquette Avenue, Suite 403
Minneapolis, MN 55401
612/333-1183

Mississippi State Bar
P.O. Box 2168
Jackson, MS 39225
601/948-4471

Missouri Bar
P.O. Box 119
Jefferson City, MO 65102
314/635-4128

State Bar of Montana
P.O. Box 577
Helena, MT 59624
406/442-7660

Nebraska State Bar Association
P.O. Box 81809
Lincoln, NE 68501
402/475-7091

State Bar of Nevada
500 South Third Street, Suite 2
Las Vegas, NV 89101
702/382-0502

New Hampshire Bar Association
112 Pleasant Street
Concord, NH 03301
603/224-6942

New Jersey State Bar Association
New Jersey Law Center
One Constitution Square
New Brunswick, NJ 08901
908/249-5000

State Bar of New Mexico
P.O. Box 25883
Albuquerque, NM 87125
505/842-6132

New York State Bar Association
One Elk Street
Albany, NY 12207
518/463-3200

North Carolina State Bar
P.O. Box 25908
Raleigh, NC 27611
919/828-4620

**State Bar Association
of North Dakota**
515 ½ East Broadway
Suite 101
Bismarck, ND 58502
701/255-1404

Ohio State Bar Association
P.O. Box 16562
Columbus, OH 43216
614/487-2050

Oklahoma Bar Association
P.O. Box 53036
Oklahoma City, OK 73152
405/524-2365

Oregon State Bar
P.O. Box 1689
Lake Oswego, OR 97035
503/620-0222

Pennsylvania Bar Association
P.O. Box 186
Harrisburg, PA 17108
717/238-6715

Puerto Rico Bar Association
P.O. Box 1900
San Juan, PR 00903
809/721-3358

Rhode Island Bar Association
115 Cedar Street
Providence, RI 02903
401/421-5740

South Carolina Bar
950 Taylor Street
Columbia, SC 29202
803/799-6653

State Bar of South Dakota
222 East Capitol
Pierre, SD 57501
605/224-7554

Tennessee Bar Association
3622 West End Avenue
Nashville, TN 37205
615/383-7421

State Bar of Texas
P.O. Box 12487
Austin, TX 78711
512/463-1463

Utah State Bar
645 South 200 East
Salt Lake City, UT 84111
801/531-9077

Vermont Bar Association
P.O. Box 100
Montpelier, VT 05601
802/223-2020

Virginia State Bar
801 East Main Street, Suite 1000
Richmond, VA 23219
804/775-0500

Virgin Islands Bar Association
P.O. Box 4108
Christiansted, VI 00822
809/778-7497

Washington State Bar Association
500 Westin Building
2001 6th Avenue
Seattle, WA 98121
206/448-0441

West Virginia State Bar
State Capitol
Charleston, WV 25305
304/348-2456

State Bar of Wisconsin
402 West Wilson
Madison, WI 53703
608/257-3838

Wyoming State Bar
P.O. Box 109
Cheyenne, WY 82003
307/632-9061

Source: American Bar Association

STATE LONG-TERM CARE OMBUDSMEN

Office of the LTC Ombudsman
3601 C. Street, Suite 260
Anchorage, AK 99503
907/563-6393

State LTC Ombudsman
770 Washington Avenue
RSA Plaza, Suite 470
Montgomery, AL 36130
205/242-5743

State LTC Ombudsman
P.O. Box 1437, Slot 1417
Little Rock, AR 72203
501/682-2441

State LTC Ombudsman
1789 West Jefferson, 950A
Phoenix, AZ 85007
602/542-4446

State LTC Ombudsman
1600 K Street
Sacramento, CA 95814
916/323-6681

State LTC Ombudsman
455 Sherman Street, Suite 130
Denver, CO 80203
303/722-0300

DC LTC Ombudsman
601 E Street NW
Fourth Floor, Building A
Washington, DC 22004
202/662-4933

State LTC Ombudsman
175 Main Street
Hartford, CT 06106
203/566-7770

State LTC Ombudsman
11-13 Church Avenue
Milford, DE 19963
302/422-1386

State LTC Ombudsman
154 Holland Building
600 South Calhoun
Tallahassee, FL 32399
904/488-6190

State LTC Ombudsman
878 Peachtree Street NE, Room 642
Atlanta, GA 30309
404/894-5336

State LTC Ombudsman
335 Merchant Street, Room 241
Honolulu, HI 96813
808/586-0100

State LTC Ombudsman
914 Grand Avenue #236
Jewett Building
Des Moines, IA 50319
515/281-5187

State Ombudsman for the Elderly
Statehouse, Room 180
Boise, ID 83720
208/334-2220

State LTC Ombudsman
421 East Capitol Avenue
Springfield, IL 62701
217/785-3143

State LTC Ombudsman
P.O. Box 7083
Indianapolis, IN 46207
317/232-7134

State LTC Ombudsman
Docking State Office Building
122 South
Topeka, KS 66612
913/296-4986

State LTC Ombudsman
275 East Main Street, Fourth Floor West
Frankfort, KY 40621
502/564-6930

State LTC Ombudsman
4550 North Boulevard, Second Floor
Baton Rouge, LA 70898
504/925-1700

Ombudsman, Legal Services for the Elderly
113 Bangor Street
P.O. Box 2723
Augusta, ME 04338
207/289-4056

State LTC Ombudsman
301 West Preston Street, Room 1004
Baltimore, MD 21201
410/225-1083

State LTC Ombudsman
1 Ashburton Place, Fifth Floor
Boston, MA 02108
617/727-7750

State LTC Ombudsman
416 North Homer Street, Suite 101
Alpha Building
Lansing, MI 48912
517/336-6753

State LTC Ombudsman
444 Lafayette Road
St. Paul, MN 55155
612/296-0382

State LTC Ombudsman
421 West Pascagoula Street
Jackson, MS 39203
601/949-2029

State LTC Ombudsman
P.O. Box 1337
Jefferson City, MO 65102
314/751-3082

State LTC Ombudsman
Room 219, Capitol Building
Helena, MT 59620
406/444-4676

State LTC Ombudsman
301 Centennial Mall South
P.O. Box 95044
Lincoln, NE 68509
402/471-2306

State LTC Ombudsman
340 North 11th Street, Suite 114
Las Vegas, NV 89101
702/486-3545

State LTC Ombudsman
6 Hazen Drive
Concord, NH 03301
603/271-4375

Office of the Ombudsman for the Institutionalized Elderly
28 West State Street
Room 305
CN 808
Trenton, NJ 08625
609/292-8016

State LTC Ombudsman
224 East Palace Avenue
Fourth Floor
La Villa Rivera Building
Santa Fe, NM 87501
505/827-7640

State LTC Ombudsman
Agency Building #2
Albany, NY 12223
518/474-7329

State LTC Ombudsman
693 Palmer Drive
Caller Box Number 29531
Raleigh, NC 27603
919/733-3983

State LTC Ombudsman
State Capitol Building
P.O. Box 7070
Bismarck, ND 58507
701/224-2577

State LTC Ombudsman
50 West Broad Street, Ninth Floor
Columbus, OH 43266
614/466-1221

State LTC Ombudsman
321 Northeast 28th Street
P.O. Box 25352
Oklahoma City, OK 73125
405/521-6734

State LTC Ombudsman
2475 Lancaster Drive NE, #B-9
Salem, OR 97310
503/378-6533

State LTC Ombudsman
231 State Street
Harrisburg, PA 17101
717/783-7247

State LTC Ombudsman
160 Pine Street
Providence, RI 02903
401/277-2858

State LTC Ombudsman
1205 Pendleton Street
308 Brown Building
Columbia, SC 29201
803/734-0546

State LTC Ombudsman
700 Governors Drive
Pierre, SD 57501
605/773-3656

State LTC Ombudsman
706 Church Street, Suite 201
Nashville, TN 37219
615/741-2056

State LTC Ombudsman
1949 South Highway 35, Third Floor
Austin, TX 78741
512/444-2727

LTC Ombudsman
120 North 200 West, Room 401
Salt Lake City, UT 84103
801/538-3910

State LTC Ombudsman
700 Centre, Tenth Floor
700 East Franklin Street
Richmond, VA 23219
804/225-2271

State LTC Ombudsman
103 South Main Street
Waterbury, VT 05671
802/241-2400

State LTC Ombudsman
12200 South 336th Street
Federal Way, WA 98003
206/838-6810

State LTC Ombudsman
214 North Hamilton Street
Madison, WI 53703
608/266-8944

State LTC Ombudsman
State Capitol Complex
Charleston, WV 25305
304/558-3317

State LTC Ombudsman
953 Water Street
Wheatland, WY 82201
307/322-5553

Source: National Citizens Coalition for Nursing Home Reform

STATE MEDICAL ASSOCIATIONS

Medical Association of the State of Alabama
19 South Jackson
P.O. Box 1900
Montgomery, AL 36102

Alaska State Medical Association
407 Laurel Street
Anchorage, AK 99508

Arizona Medical Association
810 West Bethany Home Road
Phoenix, AZ 85013

Arkansas Medical Society
P.O. Box 5776
Little Rock, AR 72215

California Medical Association
P.O. Box 7690
San Francisco, CA 94120

Colorado Medical Society
P.O. Box 17550
Denver, CO 80217

Connecticut State Medical Society
160 St. Ronan Street
New Haven, CT 06511

Medical Society of Delaware
1925 South Lovering Avenue
Wilmington, DE 19806

Medical Society of the District of Columbia
1707 L Street NW
Suite 400
Washington, DC 20036

Florida Medical Association
P.O. Box 2411
Jacksonville, FL 32203

Medical Association of Georgia
938 Peachtree Street NE
Atlanta, GA 30309

Guam Medical Society
Box 6690-C
Tamuning, Guam 96911

Hawaii Medical Association
31360 South Beretania Street, 2nd Floor
Honolulu, HI 96814

Idaho Medical Asociation
P.O. Box 2668
Boise, ID 83701

Illinois State Medical Society
20 North Michigan Avenue
Chicago, IL 60602

Indiana State Medical Association
322 Canal Walk
Indianapolis, IN 46208

Iowa Medical Society
1001 Grand Avenue
West Des Moines, IA 50265

Kansas Medical Society
1300 Topeka Avenue SW
Topeka, KS 66612

Kentucky Medical Association
301 North Hurstbourne Parkway
Suite 200
Louisville, KY 40222

Louisiana State Medical Society
3501 North Causeway Boulevard
Suite 800
Metairie, LA 70113

Maine Medical Association
P.O. Box 190
Manchester, ME 04351

Medical and Chuirgical Faculty of the State of Maryland
1211 Cathedral Street
Baltimore, MD 21201

Massachusetts Medical Society
1440 Main Street
Waltham, MA 02154

Michigan State Medical Society
P.O. Box 950
East Lansing, MI 48826

Minnesota Medical Association
2221 University Avenue SE, Suite 400
Minneapolis, MN 55414

Mississippi State Medical Association
735 Riverside
Jackson, MS 39216

Missouri Medical Association
113 Madison Street
P.O. Box 1028
Jefferson City, MO 65102

Montana Medical Association
2021 11th Avenue
Helena, MT 59601

Nebraska Medical Association
233 South 13th Street
Suite 1512
Lincoln, NE 68508

Nevada State Medical Association
3660 Baker Lane, #101
Reno, NV 89509

New Hampshire Medical Association
7 North State Street
Concord, NH 03301

Medical Society of New Jersey
2 Princess Road
Lawrenceville, NJ 08648

New Mexico Medical Society
7770 Jefferson NE, Suite 400
Albuquerque, NM 87109

Medical Society of the State of New York
420 Lakeville Road
P.O. Box 5405
Lake Success, NY 11042

North Carolina Medical Society
P.O. Box 27167
Raleigh, NC 27611

North Dakota Medical Association
P.O. Box 1198
Bismarck, ND 58502

Ohio State Medical Association
1500 Lake Shore Drive.
Columbus, OH 43204

Oklahoma State Medical Association
601 Northwest Expressway
Oklahoma City, OK 73118

Oregon Medical Association
5210 Southwest Corbett
Portland, OR 97201

Pennsylvania Medical Association
777 East Park Drive
Harrisburg, PA 17111

Puerto Rico Medical Association
P.O. Box 9387
Santurce, PR 00908

Rhode Island Medical Society
106 Francis Street
Providence, RI 02903

South Carolina Medical Association
P.O. Box 11188
Columbia, SC 29211

South Dakota State Medical Association
1323 South Minnesota Avenue
Sioux Falls, SD 57105

Tennessee Medical Association
2301 21st Avenue S
Nashville, TN 37212

Texas Medical Association
401 West 15th Street
Austin, TX 78701

U.S. Virgin Islands Medical Society
P.O. Box 5986
St. Croix, VI 00823

Utah Medical Association
540 East 5th Street
Salt Lake City, UT 84102

Vermont State Medical Society
136 Main Street, Box H
Montpelier, VT 05601

Medical Society of Virginia
4205 Dover Road
Richmond, VA 23221

Washington State Medical Association
2033 Sixth Avenue, Suite 900
Seattle, WA 98121

West Virginia State Medical Association
4307 MacCorkle Avenue SE
P.O. Box 4106
Charleston, WV 25364

State Medical Society of Wisconsin
P.O. Box 1109
Madison, WI 53701

Wyoming Medical Society
P.O. Drawer 4009
Cheyenne, WY 82003

Source: *Journal of American Medical Association* 267, no. 3. , January 15, 1992.
Copyright 1992, American Medical Assocation.

GLOSSARY

advance directive 1. A written statement in which a person, usually called the *declarant,* states wishes and instructions for medical treatment if he or she is unable to make treatment decisions. 2. A document in which a person, usually called the *principal,* appoints another person to make medical decisions if the principal is unable to do so.

advocate A person who speaks for and attempts to advance another person's interests. (Under Michigan Law, the health care proxy is called a Patient Advocate for Health Care.)

agent A health care proxy appointed through a Durable Power of Attorney for Health Care document. Called an *attorney-in-fact* in some states.

arrest See cardiac arrest and pulmonary arrest.

artificially administered nutrition or sustenance Nutrients and liquids administered through tubes to people unable to take food or fluids by mouth.

attorney-in-fact See agent.

autonomy The principle that a person has the ethical, legal, and medical right of self-determination to consent or refuse to consent to medical treatment, based on the moral principle of respect for person.

best interest The duty of a second person to act in a manner that benefits or at least prevents harm to a first person. Sometimes called the *reasonable person standard,* which means that the second person should act as a reasonable person would act in a similar situation. In medical treatment decisions, the best interest standard is applied if the first person's wishes are not known. See substituted judgment.

biomedical ethics A relatively new field, which applies principles of moral philosophy to medical decision making and other aspects of medical care.

biomedical ethics committee A group established by a hospital, nursing home, or other health care institution to address ethical dilemmas that arise within the institution. These committees provide education, develop policies related to ethical issues, and may review cases which pose ethical dilemmas for staff, patients, or families.

brain death Death, as determined by tests that show that there is no function in the entire brain, in neither the upper brain (cortex) nor the lower brain (brainstem). The brain death determination is used when a person is on a respirator and the usual determination of death, that there is neither cardiac (heart) nor respiratory (breathing) activity, cannot be applied. One situation in which the brain death determination is used is organ donation.

cardiac arrest   When the heart stops beating or the beat becomes extremely weak, irregular, and rapid (fibrillation, ventricle fibrillation). Cardiac and respiratory arrest may occur simultaneously or within minutes of each other; hence the term, *cardiopulmonary arrest.*

cardiopulmonary resuscitation (CPR)   Restoring breathing or heartbeat after either cardiac or respiratory arrest. CPR methods range from basic mouth-to-mouth breathing and chest compression to more advanced methods such as administration of electric shock to the heart, drugs, and other mechanical or chemical agents. Advanced CPR is used by paramedics if 911 is called, in an emergency room, or on a hospital ward, where it may be called *code* or *code blue.*

care plan   A plan, usually for care of people who are terminally or chronically ill, developed by doctor, nurses, and other health care providers and the patient and/or patient's surrogate. The advance directive should be used as a guide in developing the plan of care to assure that the person's autonomy is respected.

coma   Sleeplike form of unconsciousness. Can be temporary (reversible) or permanent (irreversible).

comfort care/comfort care only   A plan of care that provides for keeping a person comfortable but not providing medical care, such as CPR, artificially administered nutrition and hydration, ventilation, surgery, or any treatment not necessary for comfort.

competent/competency   Capable of exercising autonomy, of giving informed consent for medical treatment. (See informed consent.) Legally, competency means that someone is no longer of minor age and is permitted to make certain kinds of decisions, such as marrying, entering into a contract, or voting, or that someone has not been determined to be incompetent through guardianship or other court proceeding.

conservatorship   See guardianship.

declaration/declarant   A written statement of wishes for medical treatment, sometimes called a *living will,* a *directive,* or in some state living will laws, a *directive to physicians.* The person who writes the declaration is the declarant.

diagnosis   The disease or condition of a patient as determined by a physician.

dialysis   A mechanical means, using tubes inserted into blood vessels or the abdomen for removing impurities and liquids from the blood when a person's kidneys fail, either temporarily or permanently. Sometimes called *hemodialysis, kidney dialysis,* or *renal dialysis.*

directive   See declaration.

disproportionately burdensome   When the burdens of medical treatment are greater than the benefits. See due proportion.

do-not-hospitalize (DHI)   A medical order, written by a physician, stating that a patient will not be transferred from a nursing home or his or her own home, if in home care, to the hospital for medical treatment.

do-not-intubate (DNI)   A medical order, written by a physician, stating that a tube will not by inserted into the throat for the purpose of long-term assisted respiration. See respirator.

do-not-resuscitate (DNR)   See no CPR.

double effect   A principle from Roman Catholic moral theology that applies to the use of pain medication. If, for example, a physician's intention in prescribing a large dose of morphine is to control a dying person's pain but that dose results in the person's death, the act is moral, because the intent was not to cause death but to control the pain.

due proportion   As stated in the Vatican Declaration of Euthanasia, physicians are not morally obligated to provide, nor are patients morally obligated to consent to, medical procedures whose results are disproportionate (unduly burdensome) to the benefits that can be expected. Some disproportionate results or undue burdens include imposing strain or suffering on the patient or imposing excessive expense on the family or community.

durable power of attorney (DPA)   A means by which a person, called the principal, can give another person power to act on behalf of the principal. All states have DPA laws and forms, which may be used to appoint a health care agent, although a DPAHC, which is specific for health care decisions, generally provides more protection for the principal.

durable power of attorney for health care (DPAHC)   A means by which one person, the principal, can appoint, by a written document, a second person, the *attorney-in-fact* or *agent,* to make health care decisions when the principal is unable to do so. Some states have DPAHC laws, including specific forms to use.

ethics committee   See biomedical ethics committee.

euthanasia   An act to cause death directly, sometimes called *mercy killing.* The intent is to cause a "good death."

gastrostomy   A surgical procedure to insert a feeding tube (gastrostomy tube) through the abdomen into the stomach. Jejunostomy and ileostomy, less frequently used, are similar procedures used to insert tubes into the small intestine.

guardianship   A legal procedure by which the court appoints a guardian for a person *(ward)* whom the court has determined to be incapable of making decisions, either for financial management or personal care or both. The amount of power granted to the guardian is determined by the court.

health care proxy   A person designated by another person, the declarant or principal, to make health care decisions when the declarant/principal is no longer able to make decisions.

hospice care   A type of care for dying people in which all of the physical, mental, and emotional needs of the patient and loved ones are attended to. Hospice care may be provided in the home, hospital, or other setting, usually during the last six months of life but possibly longer. Many hospice programs do not limit care to patients with cancer.

informed consent   Based on the principle of autonomy, informed consent means that a person or the person's surrogate must consent to medical treatment. Physicians should inform the person/surrogate of the benefits and risks of the treatment. The person must be able to receive information and be able to make a decision regarding whether to consent to or refuse the treatment. If not, the surrogate should make the decision.

intravenous (IV)   The provision of fluid, medication, and nutrients by a tube inserted into a vein. Usually intravenous therapy is not suitable for long-term administration.

intubate   To insert a tube, called an *endotracheal tube* into the throat to attach a person to a respirator. See do-not-intubate and respirator.

least restrictive alternative   As applied to medical treatment, the use of the treatment that is least invasive and minimizes the restrictions placed on the patient. Requires health care providers to consider alternatives to physical and chemical restraints, tube feeding, and other restrictive treatments

life-sustaining treatment   Sometimes called *life-prolonging* or *life-support* treatment, it refers to any medical treatment necessary to keep a person alive. Usually applied to treatments such as respirators, dialysis, and artificially administered nutrition and hydration, which are sometimes called *extraordinary,* a term to avoid.

living trust   A financial document by which a person (donor) places money and property into a trust and appoints another person or persons to serve as *trustee(s).* The trustee(s) can use and administer the estate (trust) immediately when the donor dies or becomes incompetent. Trusts can be revocable or irrevocable, depending upon the wishes of the donor. A living trust is not the same as a living will.

living will   See declaration.

Medicaid   A federal program that pays for medical care for people with limited incomes.

Medicare   The federal health insurance program for people 65 years and older and for some people with renal (kidney) disease. Medicare Part A pays part of the cost of hospital care, hospice care, and a limited amount of skilled nursing care. Part B pays part of the cost of medical (physician) care.

medigap   An informal term for the difference between what Medicare pays and the actual cost of the care provided. Sometimes applied to insurance policies intended to bridge that gap.

nasogastric (NG) tube   A feeding tube inserted through the nose into the stomach.

no CPR   A medical order, written by a physician, stating that in the event of cardiac or respiratory arrest, cardiopulmonary resuscitation will not be initiated. Sometimes called *DNR,* do-not-resuscitate.

no presumption   A term, which appears in the living will laws of many states, meaning that health care providers are not to make any presumption about a person's wishes regarding life-sustaining treatment if the person does not have a living will or other advance directive.

patient representative   A hospital staff person, whose duty is to serve as a patient advocate, assisting patients and families and helping to resolve conflict. Not the same as a Patient Advocate for Health Care (Michigan) or a health care proxy.

Patient Self-Determination Act   A federal law, effective December 1991, that requires hospitals, nursing homes, home health and hospice care providers, and health maintenance organizations (HMOs) to ask people admitted for care if they have an advance directive. If so, the directive must be placed in the person's medical record. These health providers must also provide information about state law on advance directives and about their own policies related to patients' rights to make medical decisions, and provide community education about advance directives. They cannot discriminate on the basis of whether a person has or does not have a directive.

permanent unconsciousness   A condition in which the brain is irreversibly damaged so that a person is unable to perform any conscious action such as thinking, talking, walking, eating, or feeling pain or other sensation or emotion. May range from a constant sleep-like state, sometimes called *irreversible coma,* to PVS, depending upon the extent of brain damage. Permanent unconsciousness is not the same as brain death.

persistent vegetative state (PVS)   A condition caused by disease or injury in which the upper portion of the brain has been destroyed. A person in PVS has lost all conscious function but may still have sleep/wake cycles, and there can be involuntary, repetitive arm and leg movements. The lower part of the brain, the brainstem, still functions, so breathing and heartbeat continue.

physician   A doctor of medicine.

prognosis   The probable outcome of a person's illness or injury, based on medical judgment and experience.

proxy   See health care proxy.

pulmonary arrest   Cessation of breathing or extreme difficulty in breathing which may lead to stoppage. See cardiac arrest.

qualified patient   A term used in living will laws to describe someone who has made an advance directive and has been determined by a physician (some states require two physicians) to be in a terminal condition.

rehabilitation/rehabilitative theory   Therapies designed to restore function after an illness such as a stroke or an injury. Includes assessment of degree of damage and potential for recovery, hearing and vision assessment and treatment, and physical, occupational, respiratory, and speech therapy.

respirator   A machine that takes over the breathing function by pumping air in and out of the lungs. For long-term mechanical respiration, a tube may be inserted into the throat (tracheostomy); for short-term assisted breathing, an endotracheal tube may be used. See intubate.

resuscitation   See cardiopulmonary resuscitation.

substituted judgment   A term used when making medical decisions for another, based on the principle of autonomy. It means to decide as the person would have decided for himself or herself, if he or she were able to do so. By honoring an advance directive, the health care proxy is exercising substituted judgment and respecting the declarant's right of self-determination.

surrogate   A substitute. A health care proxy, agent, or attorney-in-fact is a surrogate decision maker.

terminal condition/illness   An illness or injury from which there is no hope of recovery and for which death is the expected result. A living will does not go into effect until a person is in a terminal condition, which is defined differently in the various state living will laws.

tracheostomy   A tube inserted into the windpipe and attached to a respirator.

tube feeding   See artificially administered nutrition and hydration.

ventilator   See respirator.

ward   A person under guardianship. Called *conservatee* in some states.

will/last will and testament   A legal document stating how a person's estate (money and property) is to be distributed after the person's death. Not the same as a living will.

INDEX

Also of interest to you from Business One Irwin . . .

SOONER THAN YOU THINK
Mapping a Course For a Comfortable Retirement
Gordon K. Williamson

Overcome the confusion involved in retirement planning! Packed with useful charts, checklists, warnings, pro and con lists, fill-in timelines, and information sources, this is an essential guide for anyone concerned with future financial security. You'll understand how to challenge insurance sales pitches to ensure you are getting exactly what you need, how to prepare for shortcomings in social security and medical coverage, and much more. Also includes a unique tickler system that alerts you when an important decision needs to be made.

(275 pages)

ISBN: 1-55623-541-0

THE COMMON SENSE GUIDE TO ESTATE PLANNING
Robert H. Runde and J. Barry Zischang

Estate planning is not just for the very wealthy; tax and legal issues affect all financial transfers—no matter what the dollar amount. This helpful reference takes you step-by-step through the difficult process of naming executors, choosing a will or a living trust, determining the value of an estate, calculating the needs of survivors, selecting professional advisors, understanding tax issues, and choosing appropriate insurance providers. Includes a special section for small business owners.

(275 pages)

ISBN: 1-55623-678-6

HOW TO SELECT TOP-PERFORMING MUTUAL FUND INVESTMENTS
Aaron H. Coleman and David H. Coleman
Published by International Information Associates, Inc./U.S. Distribution by Business One Irwin.

Know the mutual fund winners from the losers! This book offers several different market timing models so you can choose the one that meets your current investment level and goals. Inside, you'll find guidelines for achieving investment goals, from retirement planning and college expense funds to major purchases such as a house or an automobile. This guide also includes actual data showing fund performance from 1976 through December 31, 1992, so you can clearly understand how timing models work.

(200 pages)

ISBN: 0-945510-14-4

SOLVING THE WORK/FAMILY PUZZLE
Bonnie Michaels with Elizabeth McCarty

This reference can rescue you from the frustrations of juggling work and family responsibilities. You'll find creative ways to balance your work and professional lives, including how to cope with guilt, communicate effectively, and organize your life to eliminate unnecessary stress. Includes a special section for single parents and parents that travel.

(288 pages)

ISBN:—1-55623-627-1

Available in fine bookstores and libraries everywhere.